AF469068

GALAPAGOS BIRDS

A PHOTOGRAPHIC VOYAGE

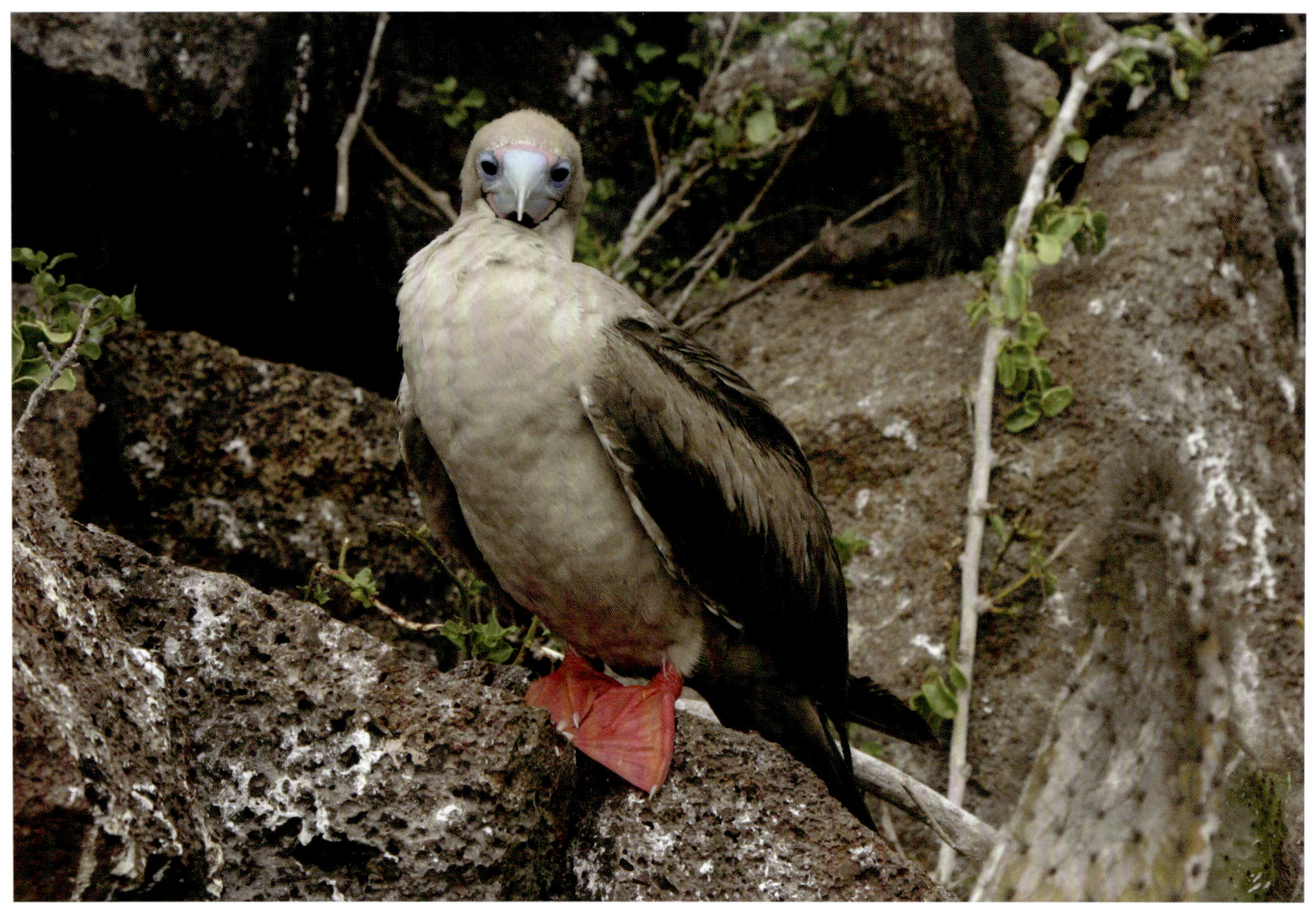

GALAPAGOS BIRDS

A PHOTOGRAPHIC VOYAGE

Mathew Tekulsky

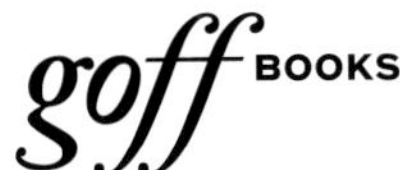

To my mother, Patience Fish Tekulsky.

We traveled the Galapagos together.

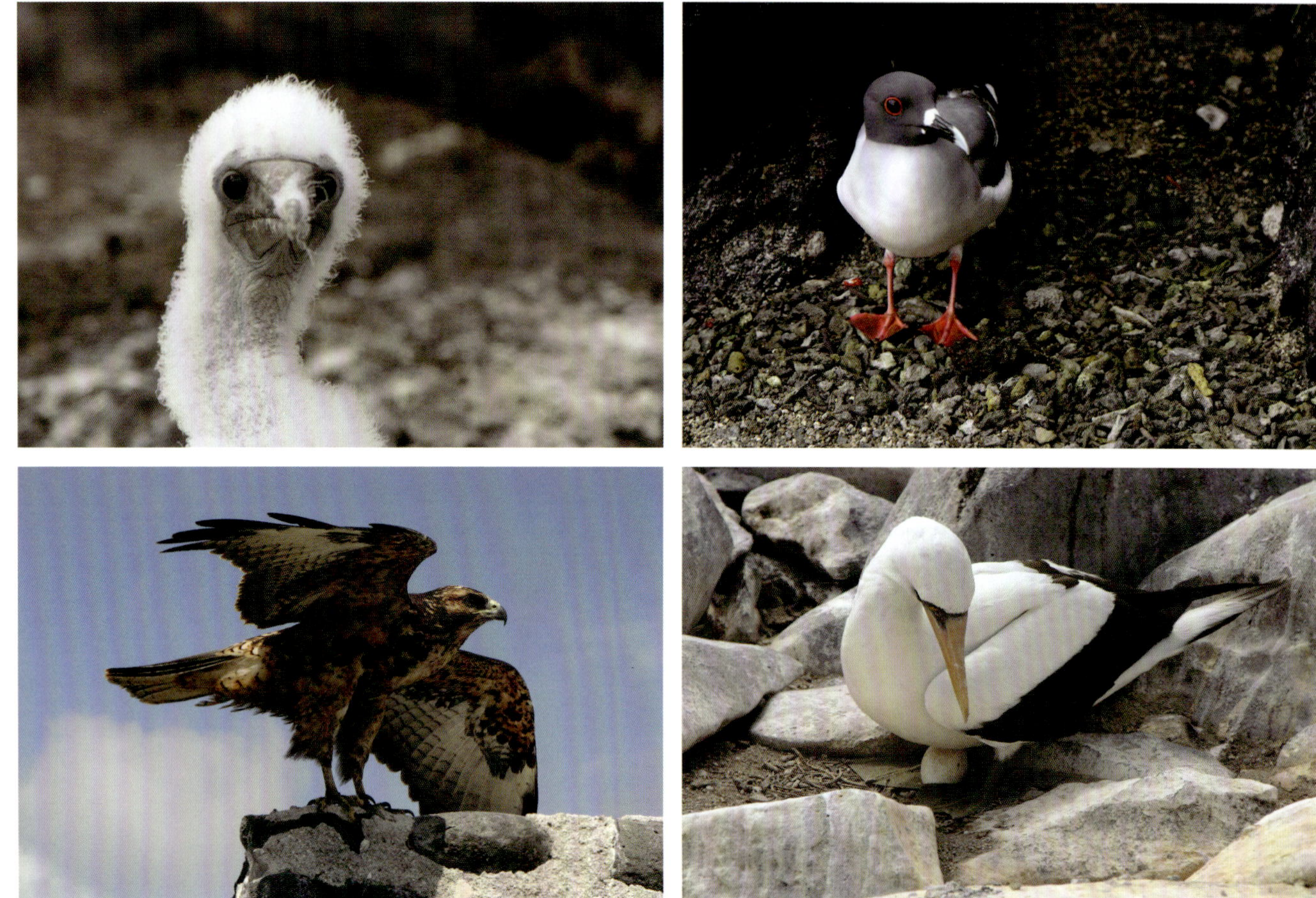

Contents

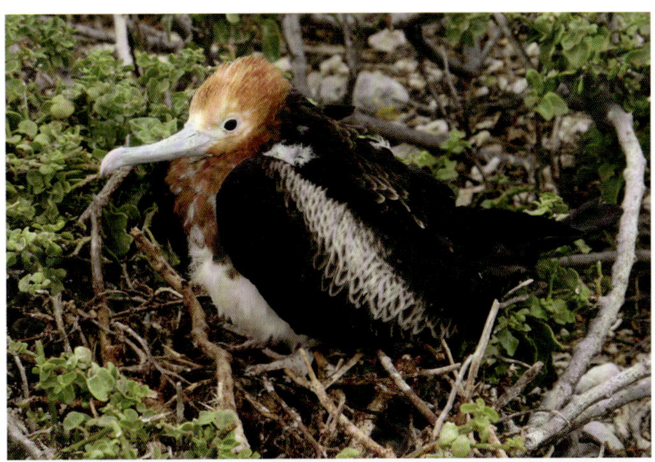

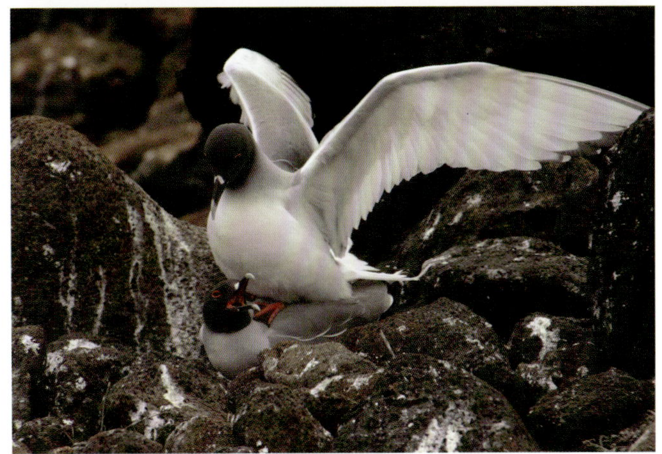

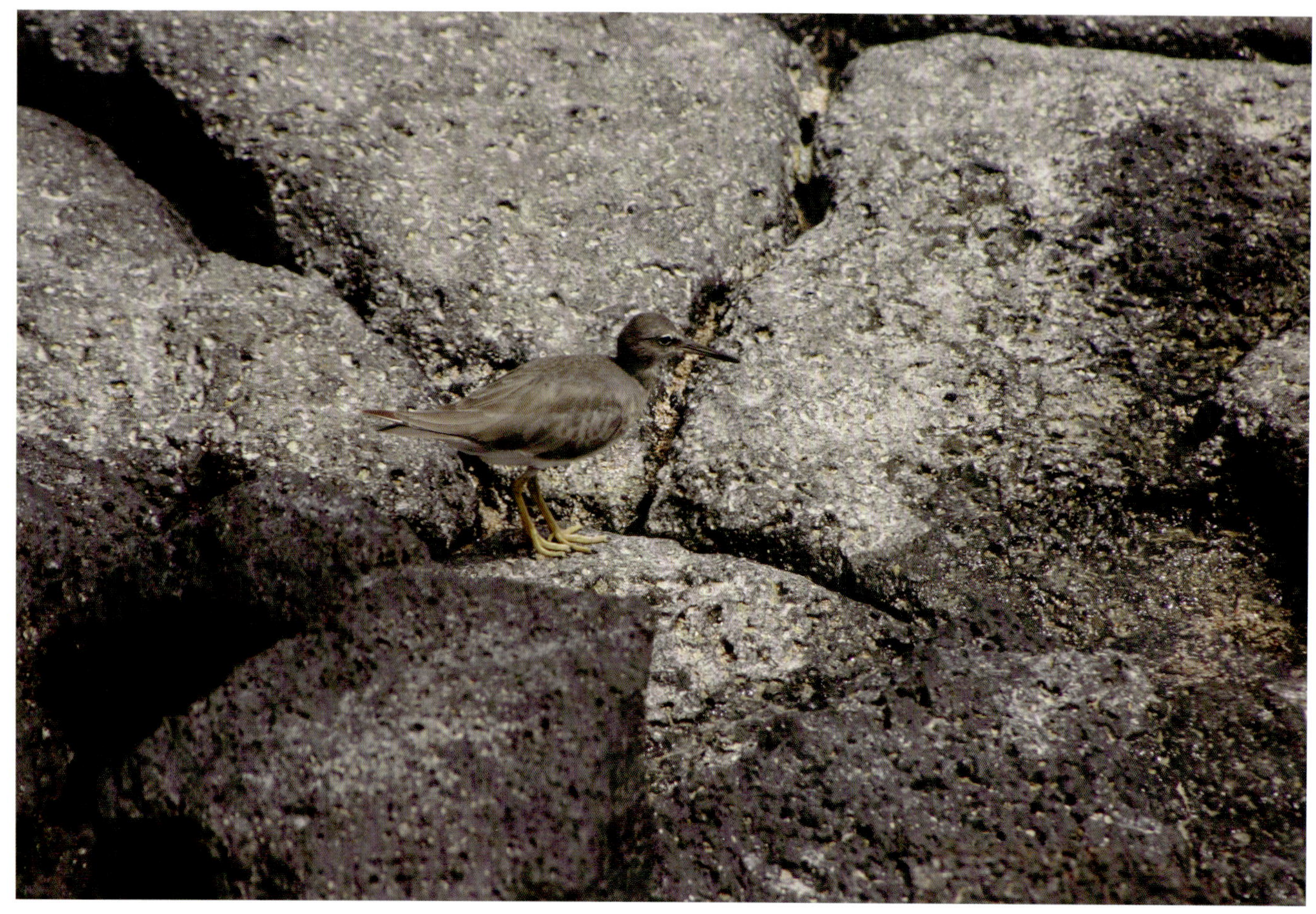

Wandering Tattler

Far, far away, on enchanted islands,
the birds of the Galapagos
wake up to greet another day.

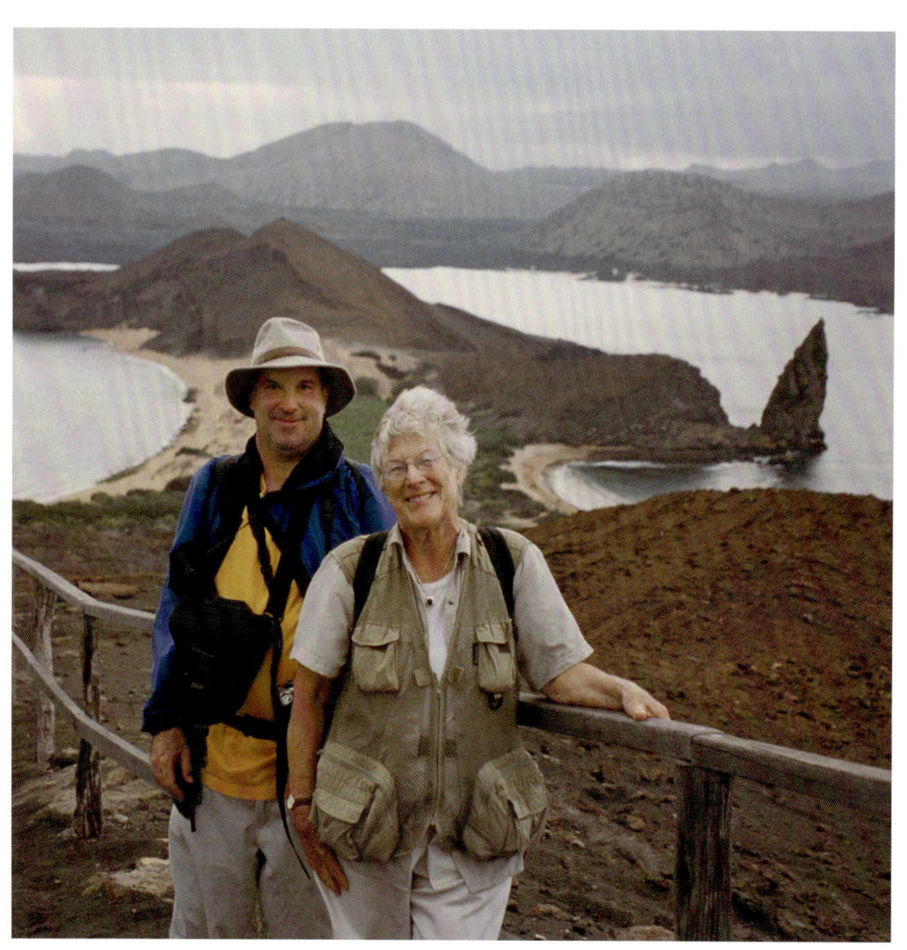

Patience Fish Tekulsky and Mathew Tekulsky, Bartolome Island, 12/23/04

Introduction

While I have spent much of my career photographing birds in my backyard in the Brentwood Hills of Los Angeles, I had the opportunity in 2004 to travel to the Galapagos Islands and photograph their native and migratory birds. As the author of the NationalGeographic.com column "The Birdman of Bel Air," which featured essays and photographs about my birding experiences both in my backyard, as well as in locations such as Yosemite, Zion, and Bryce Canyon National Parks, I figured it would be only appropriate to take on the role of world traveler, camera in hand, in the Galapagos. It was a quest that I relished, a quest for bird images and for experiences of the sort that Charles Darwin had during his 1835 visit to these magical islands, where he developed his theory elucidated in *On the Origin of Species*.

Introduction

As it happened, 2004 was the year of my fiftieth birthday, and my mother, Patience Fish Tekulsky, offered the Galapagos trip to me as a birthday gift. Needless to say, I jumped at the opportunity. After flying from Los Angeles to Miami and then to Quito, Ecuador, Mom and I flew to Guayaquil and on to San Cristobal Island, our first stop on our Galapagos voyage. There, we met up with our boat and for the next week, this vessel carried about twenty or so fellow travelers and ourselves from island to island encountering Galapagos birds of various shapes, sizes, and colors, along with the famous iguanas, lizards, sea lions, turtles, and giant tortoises.

Unlike most wild birds, the birds of the Galapagos are not afraid of people, and they remain where they happen to be, even if you approach within a few feet of them. Imagine standing right next to a Red-footed or Blue-footed Booby, or even a Magnificent Frigatebird, that doesn't even move an inch; or observing a Yellow Warbler hitching a ride on the back of a Galapagos Giant Tortoise; or witnessing the courtship ritual of the Waved Albatross, just a stone's throw away from you. These are the very bird species that Darwin would have seen all those years ago, in particular the Galapagos finches which helped him devise his theory of evolution based in part on the various shapes and sizes of these birds' beaks.

As much of my artistic life has been dedicated to photographing and writing about birds, I view this book as an opportunity to use my photographs of the Galapagos birds as a statement about how important it is to preserve our world's natural environment, including the numerous species of plants and animals that inhabit the Earth along with us humans.

I consider this book as a tribute to my mother, who loved life and nature, and who passed on her love of both to me.

LOS ANGELES, 2020

PHOTOGRAPIC VOYAGE

The Red-footed Boobies perch together as the day begins.

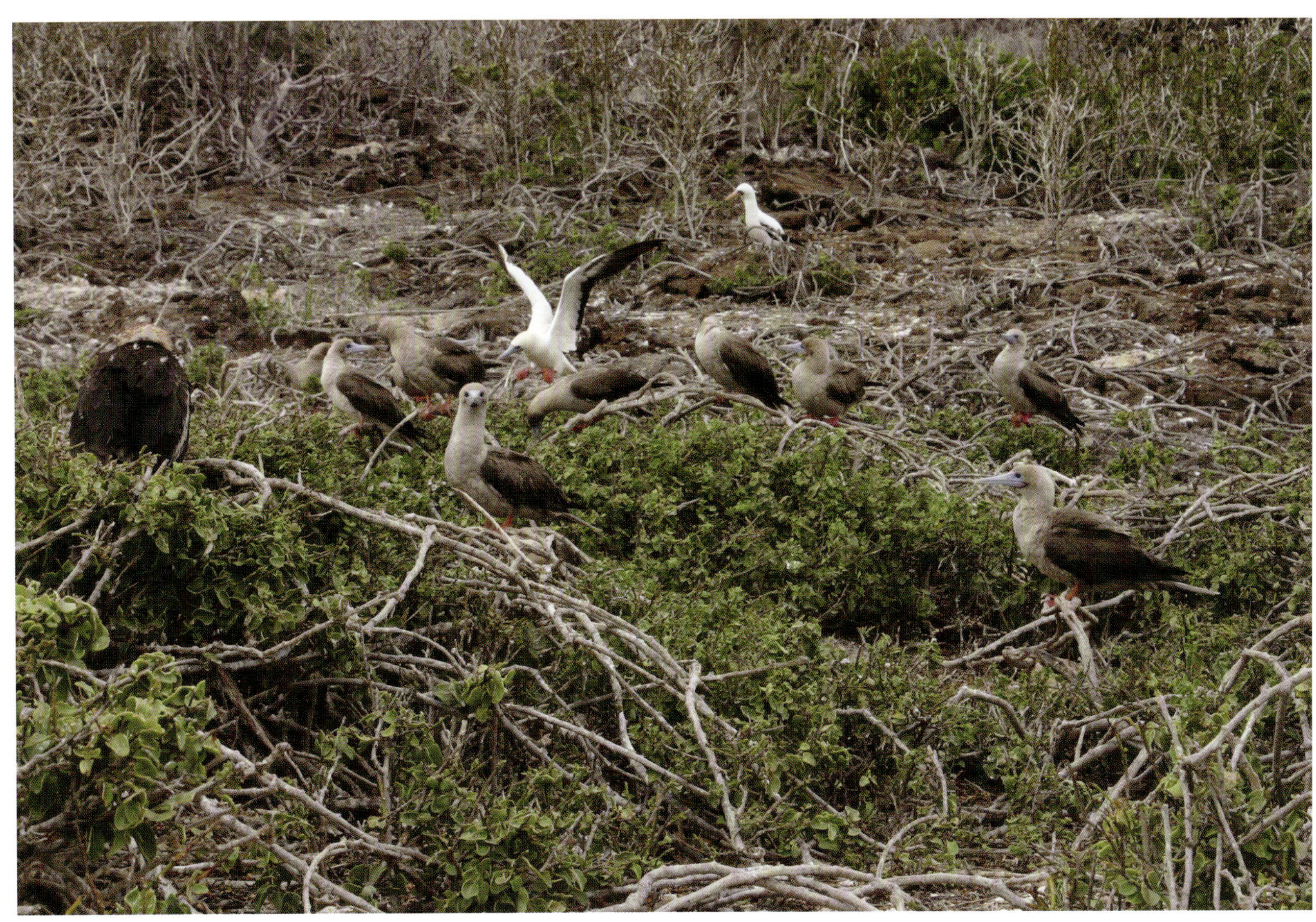

This Red-footed Booby shelters her tiny chick from the hot sun.

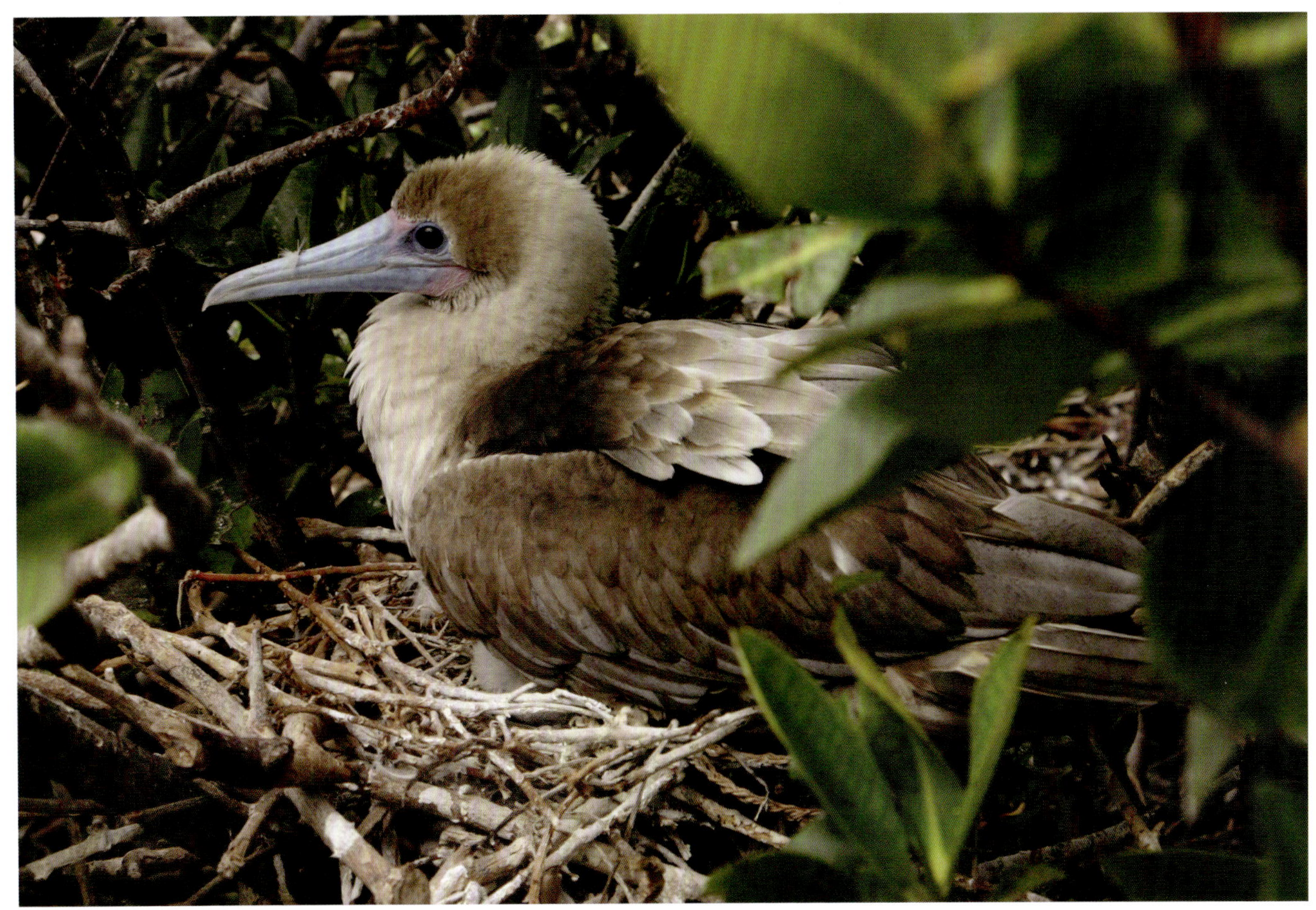

The juvenile Red-footed Booby has brown feet.

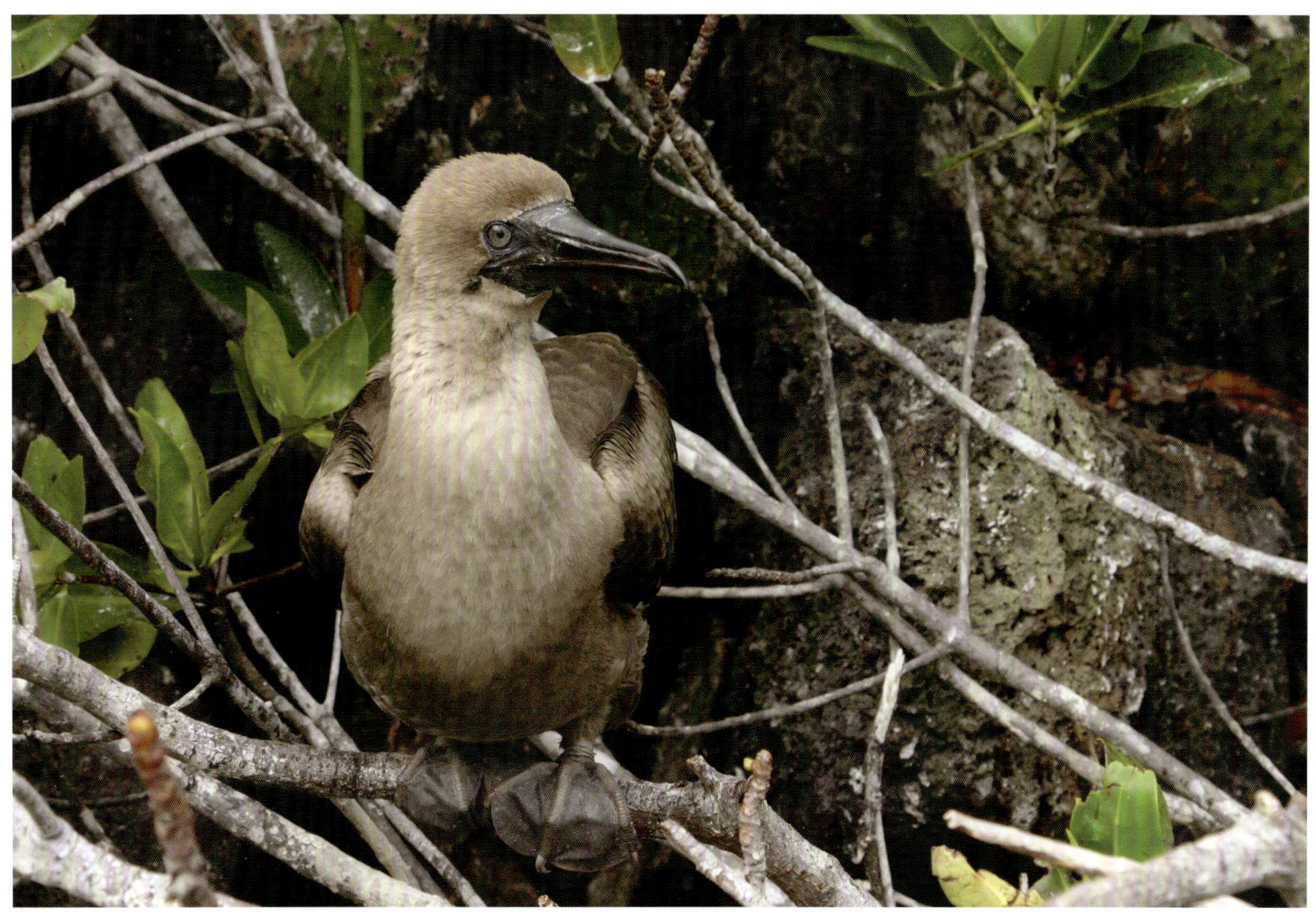

But when he grows up, his feet will turn red.

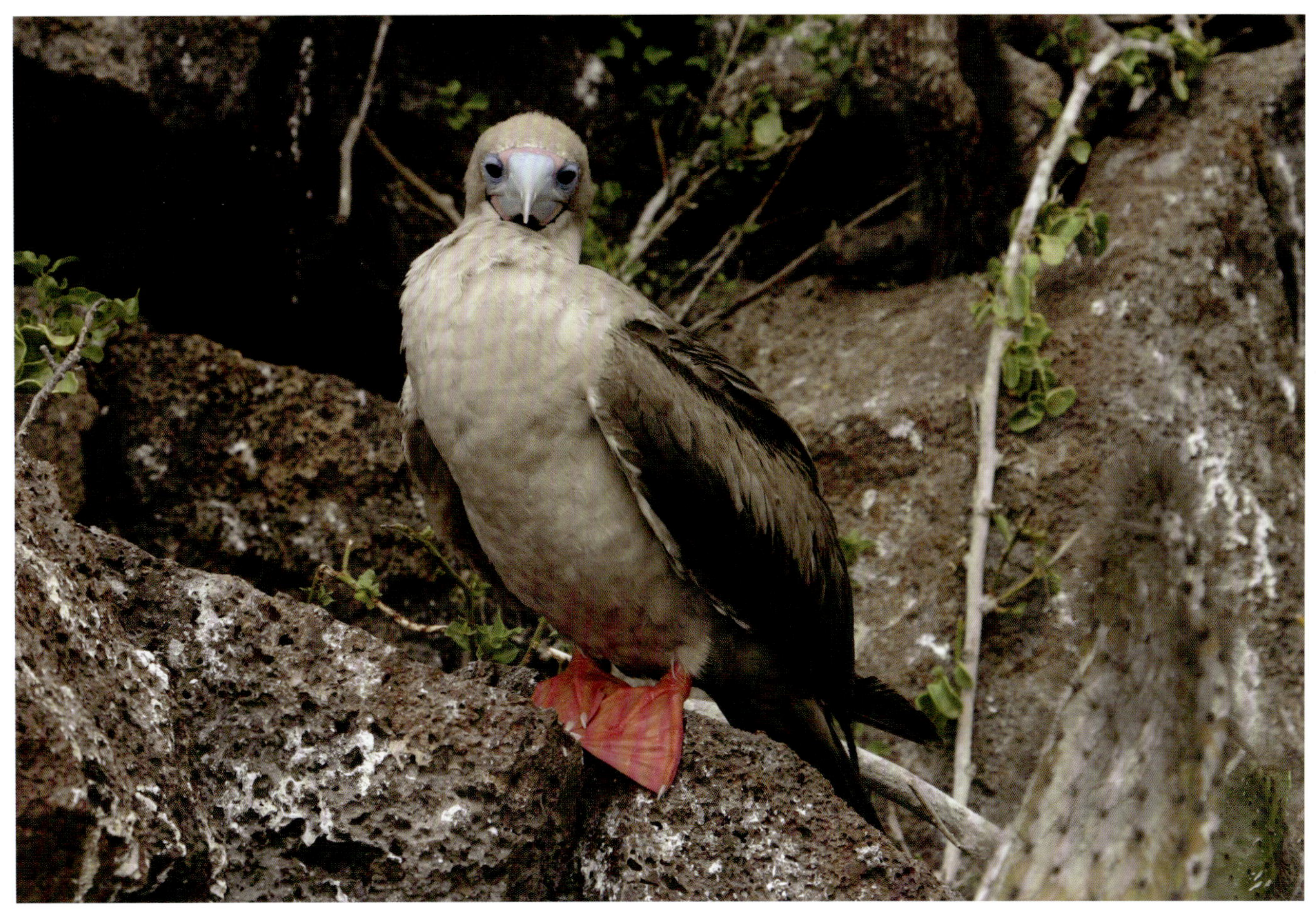

The juvenile Blue-footed Booby has grayish feet.

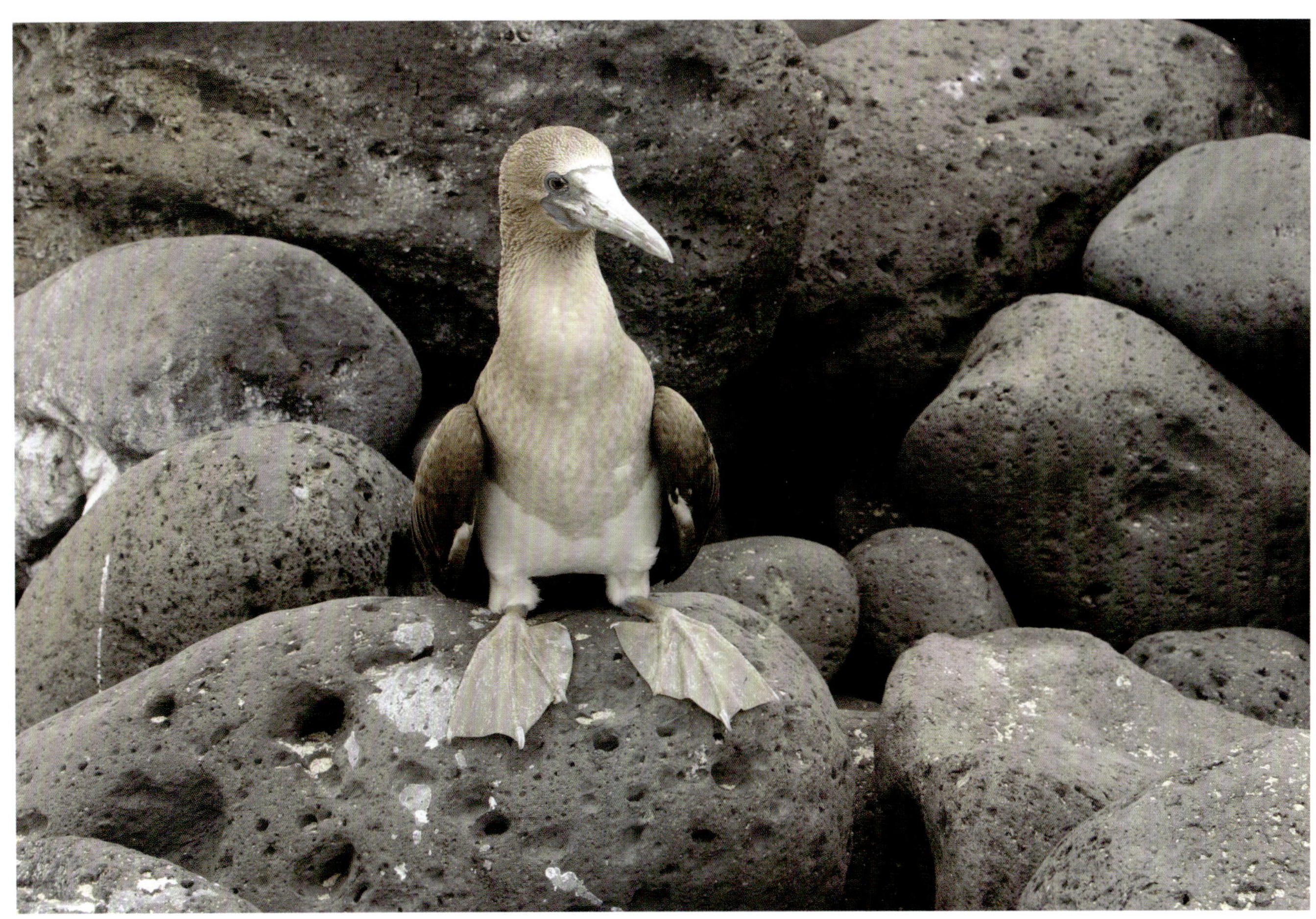

But when he grows up, his feet turn blue.

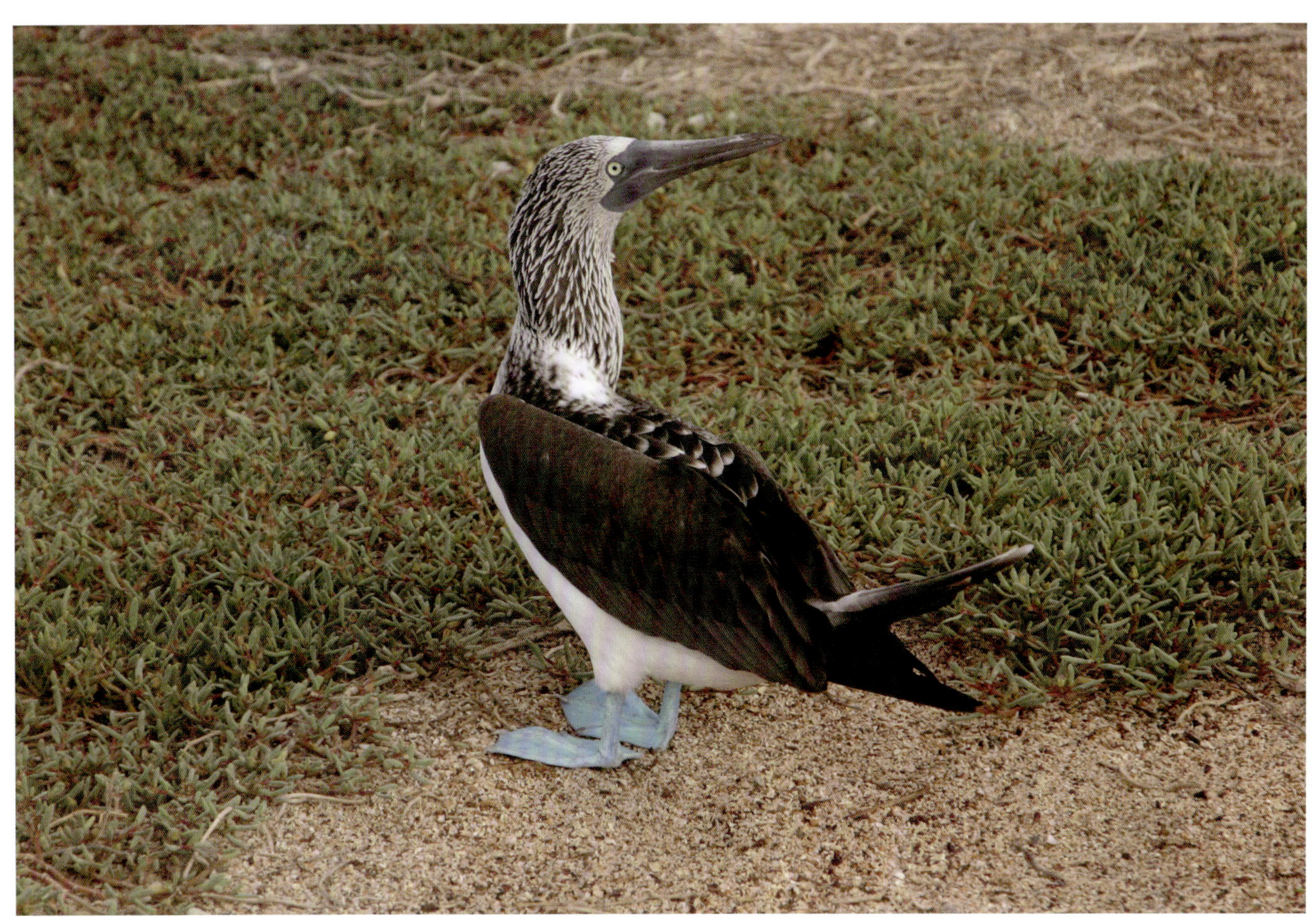

These Blue-footed Boobies gather together in a field.

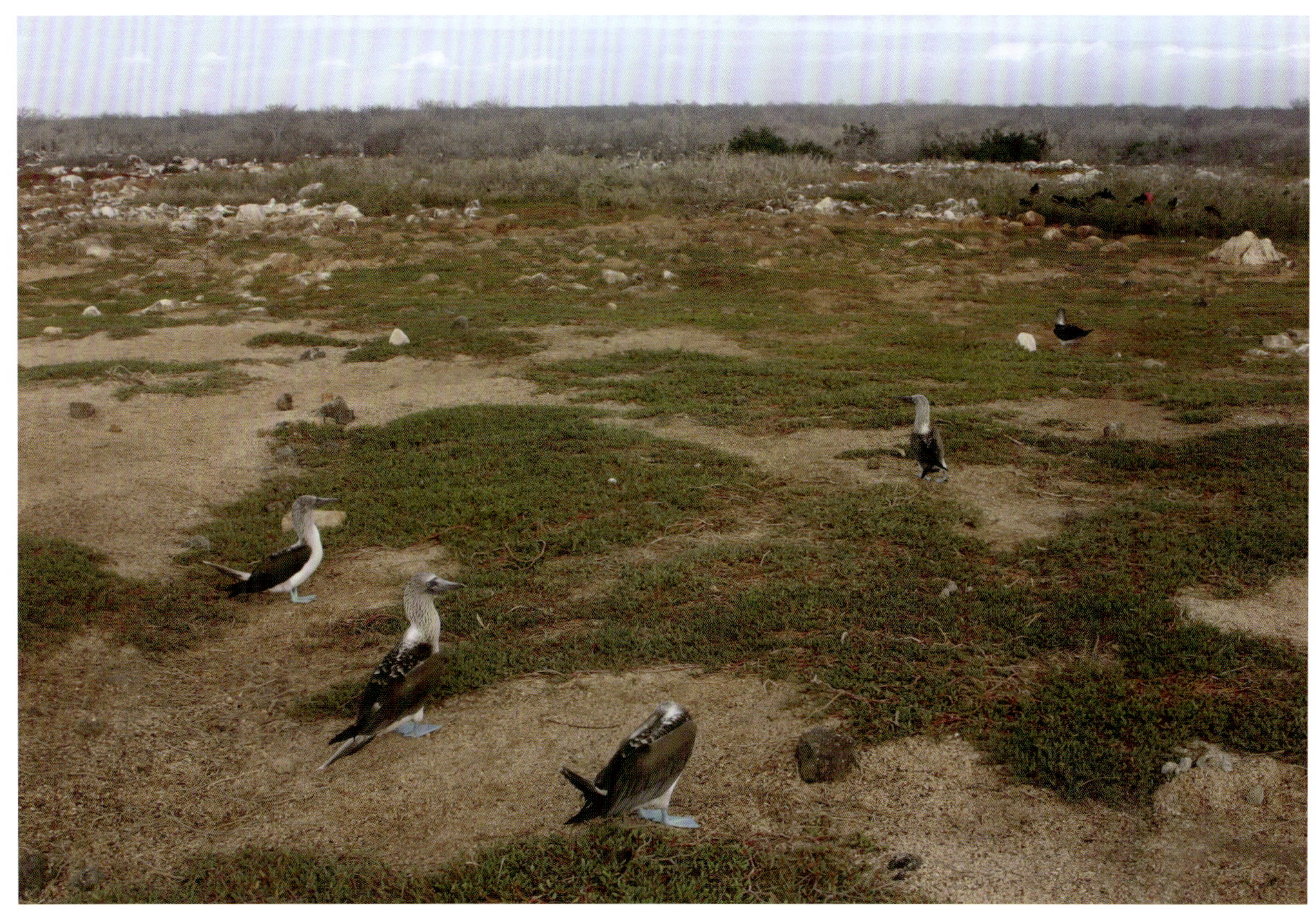

And these Blue-footed Boobies are kissing—how cute.

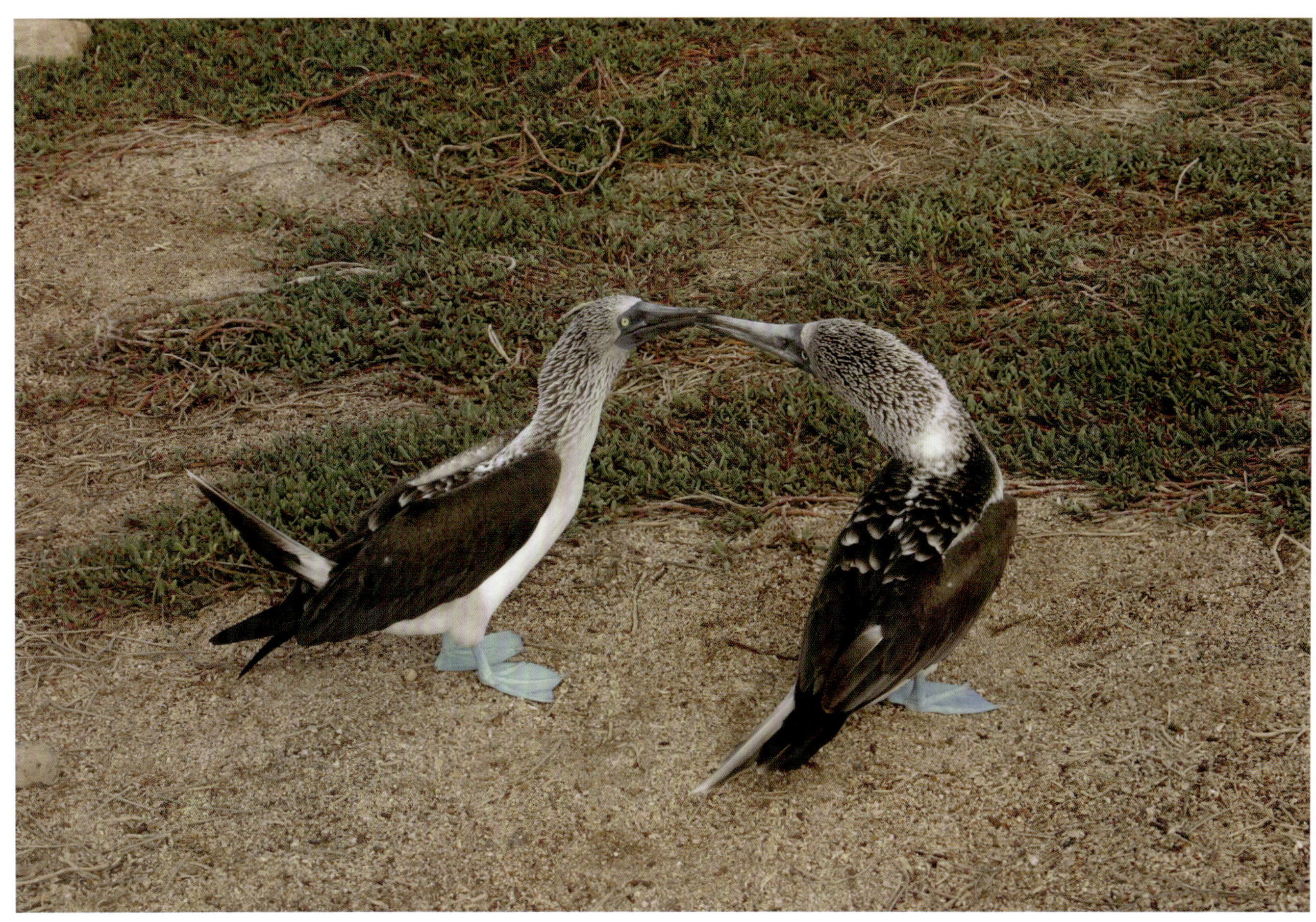

The Nazca Boobies rest on the shore.

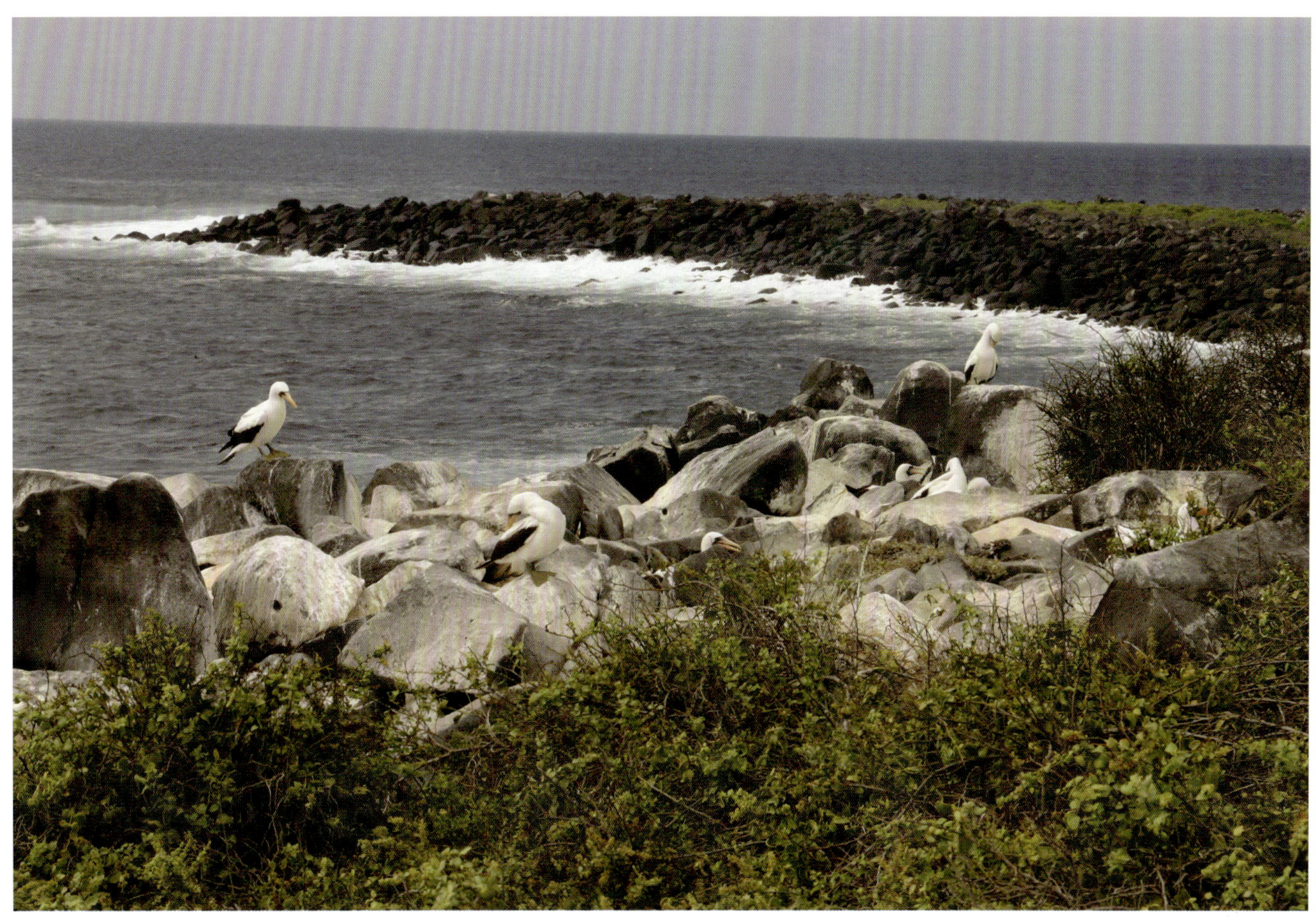

This Nazca Booby has lost her egg.

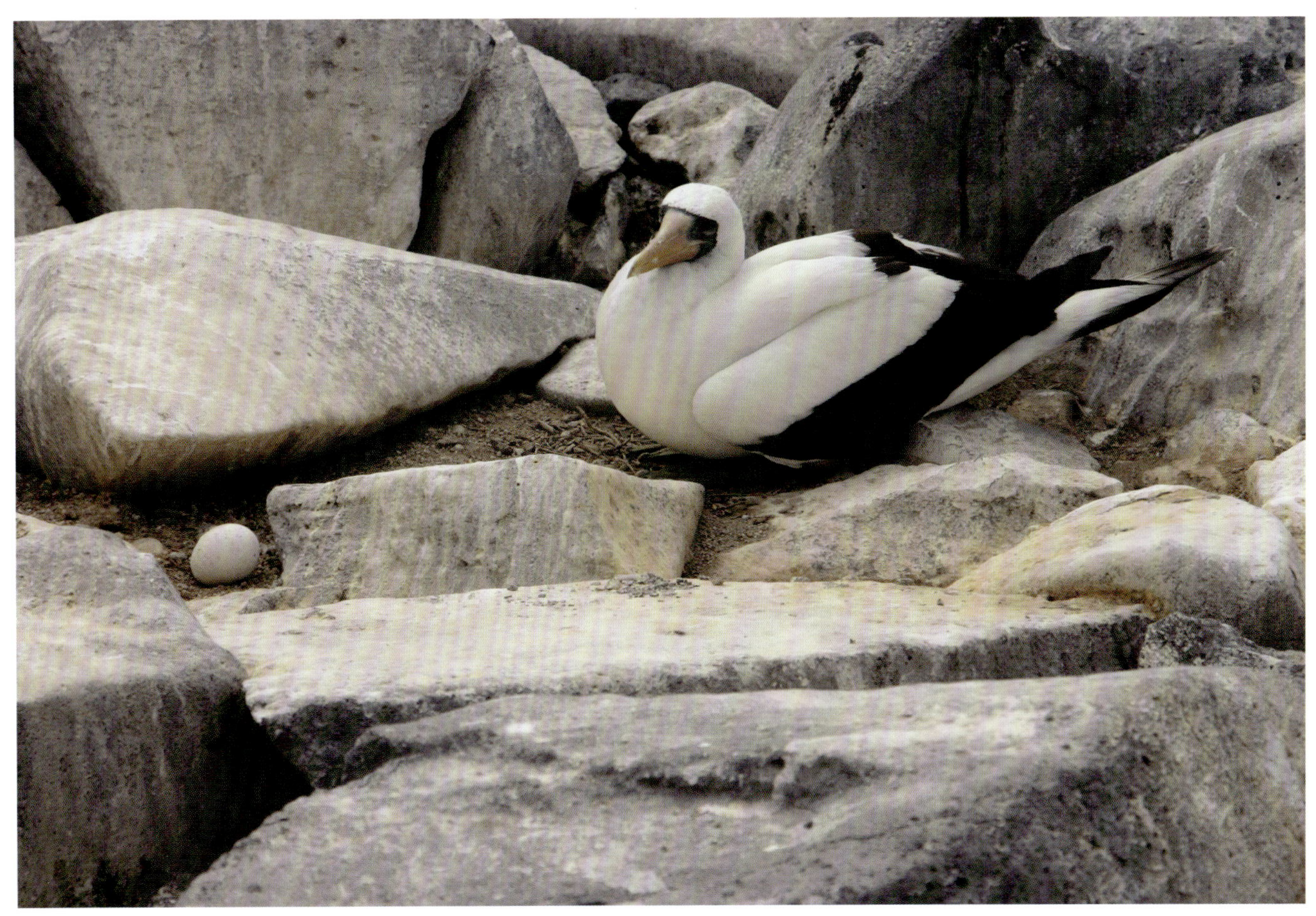

But she finds it.

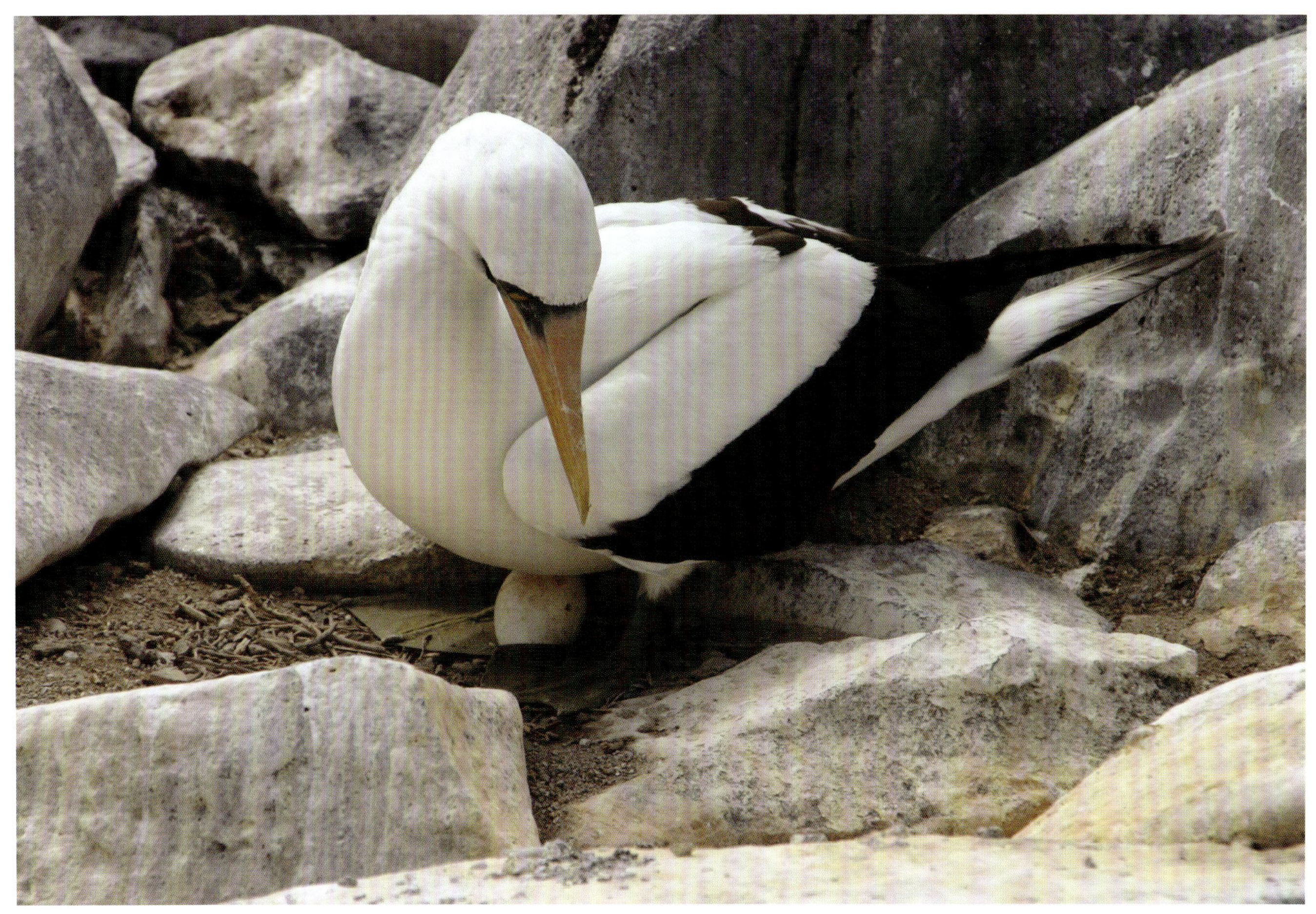

Soon, a Nazca Booby chick appears.

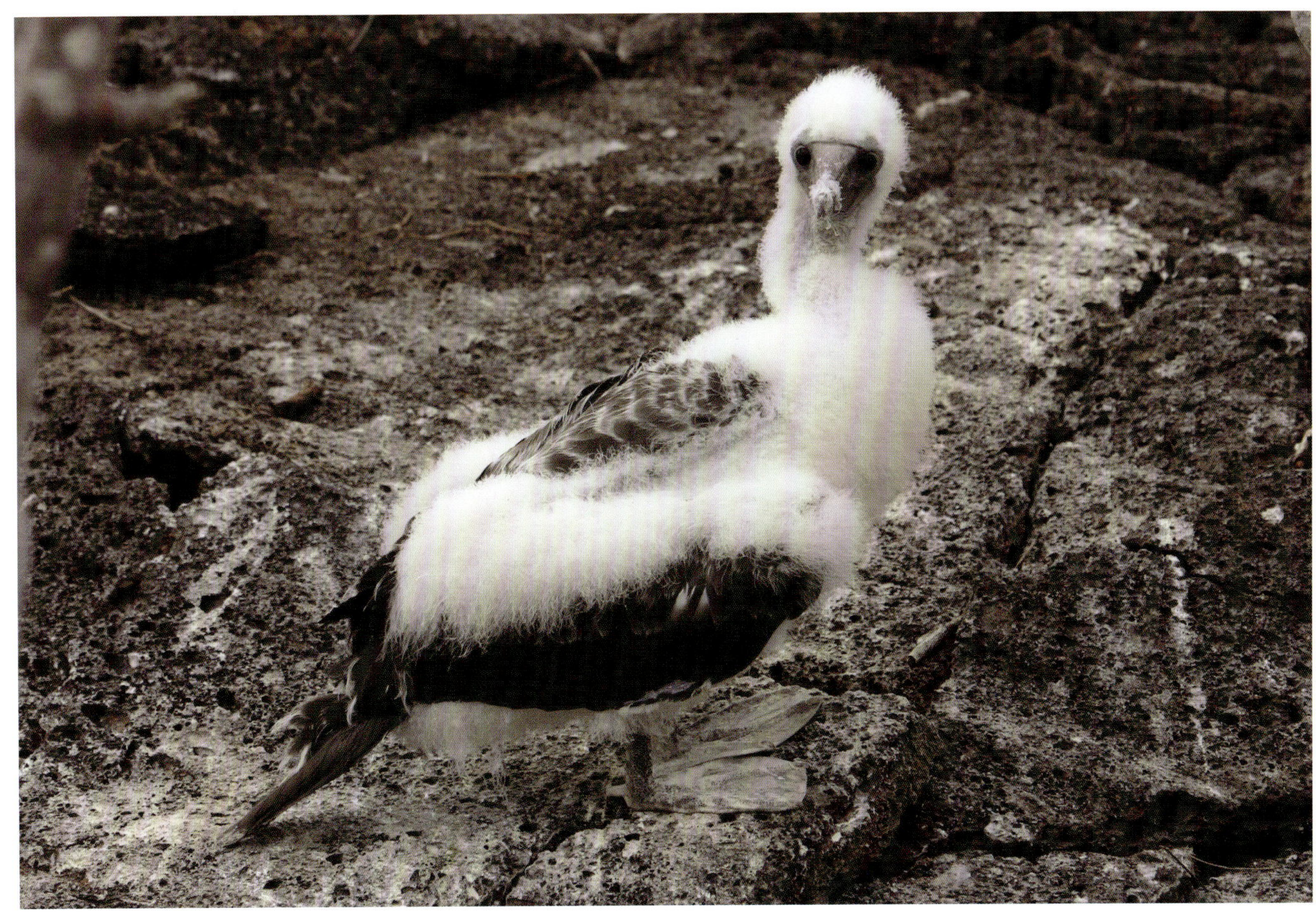

His head is covered with fluffy feathers, and he has big eyes.

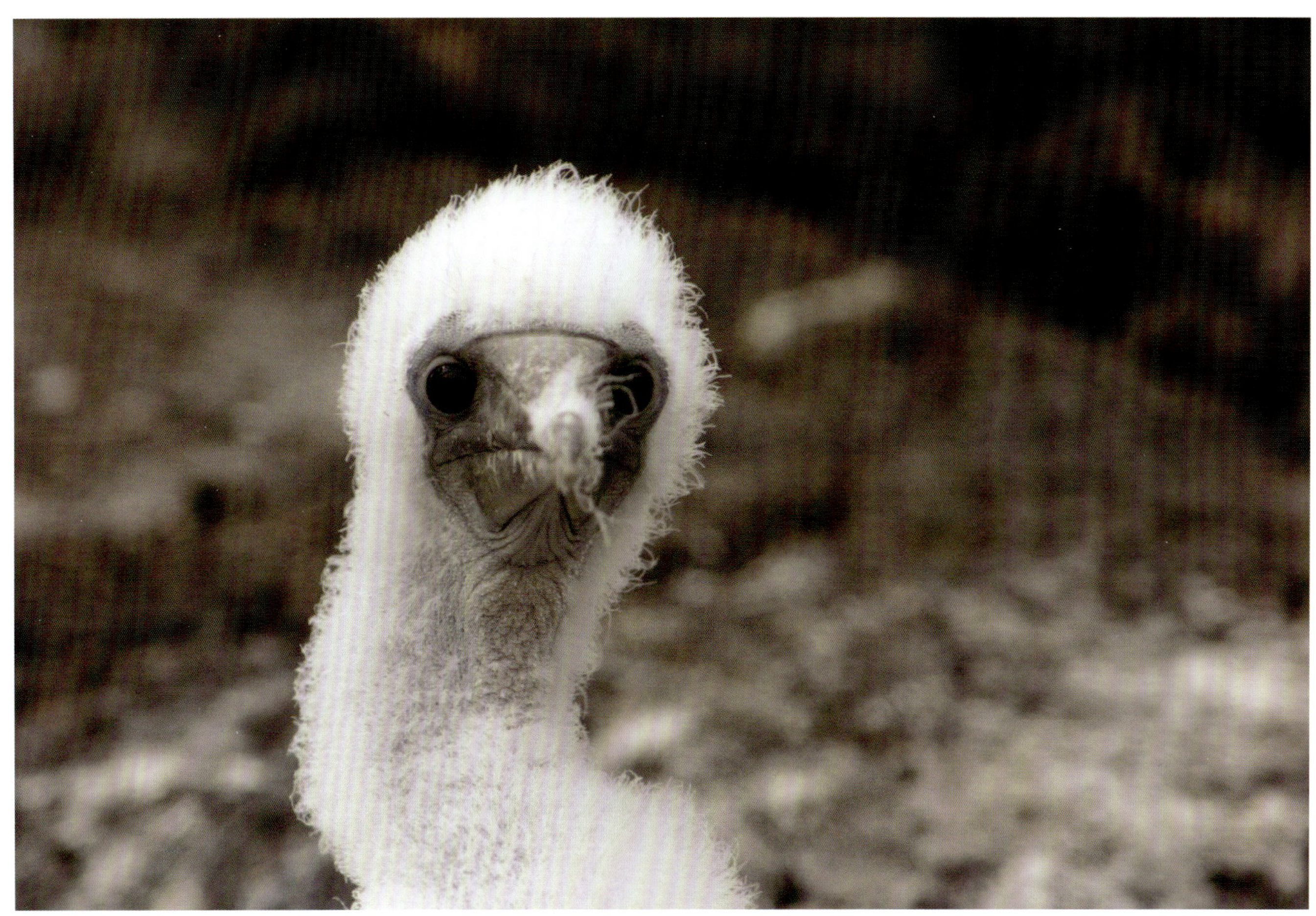

The male Magnificent Frigatebird inflates his pouch.

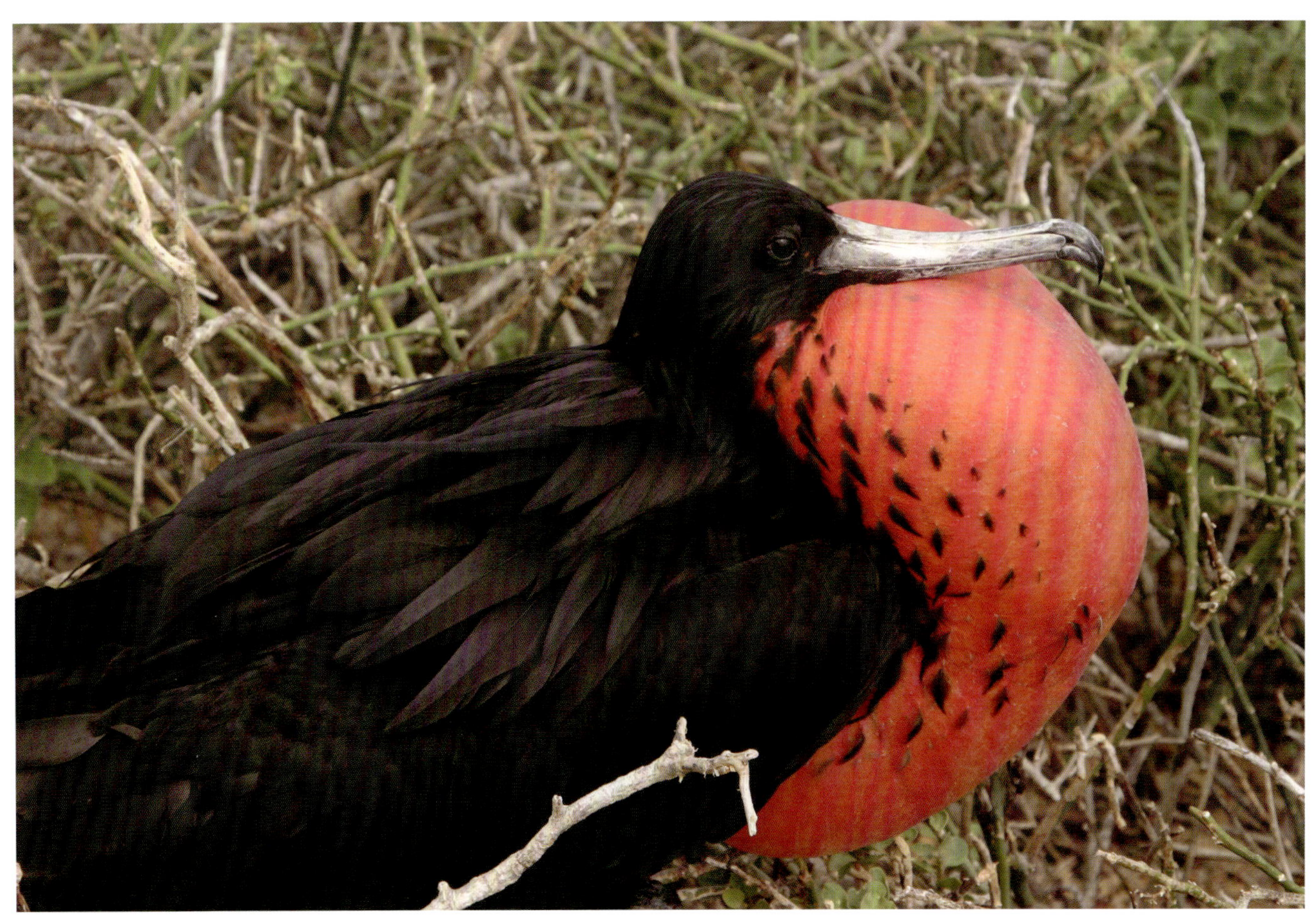

Soon, he attracts a mate.

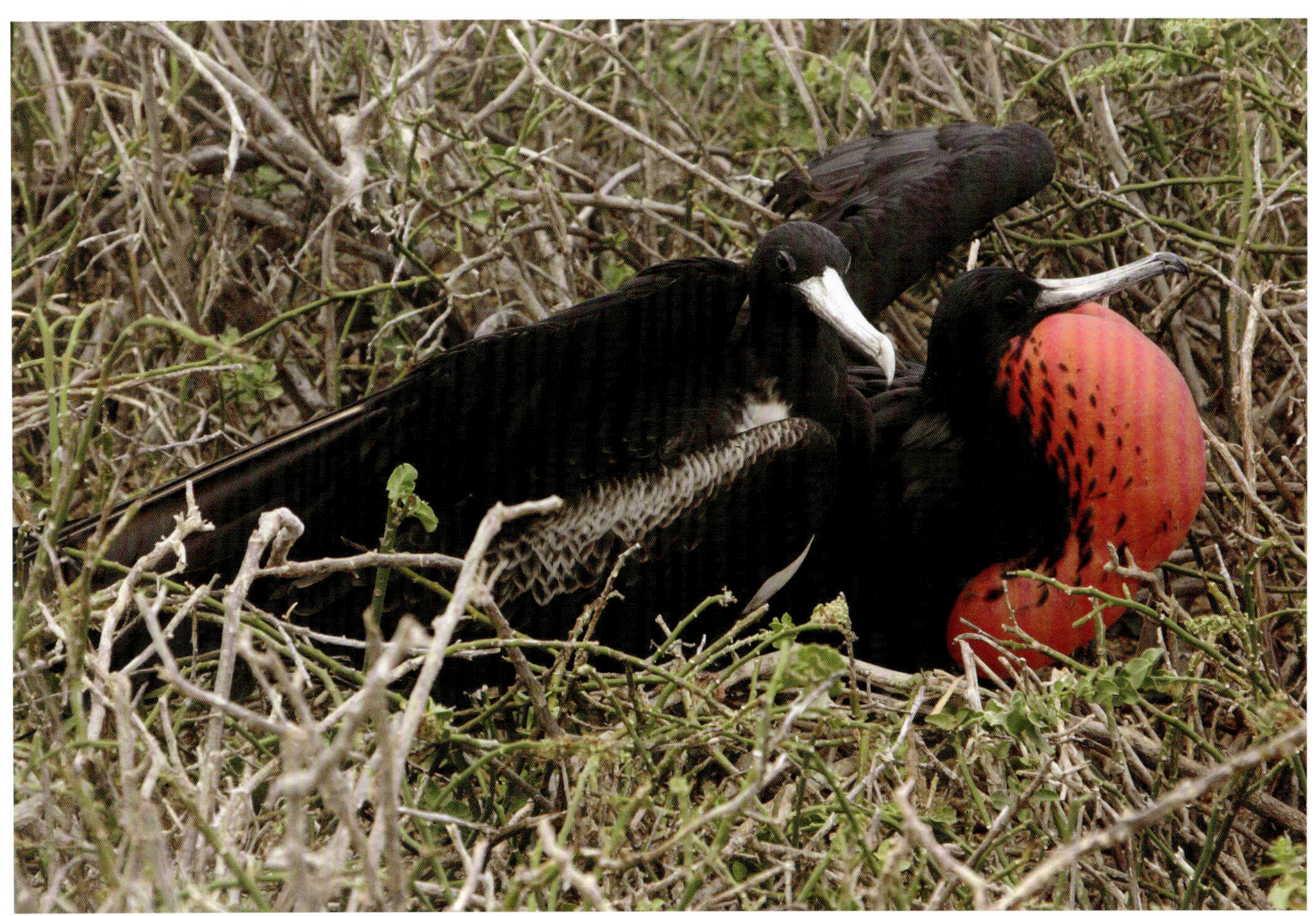

And then, a Magnificent Frigatebird chick appears.

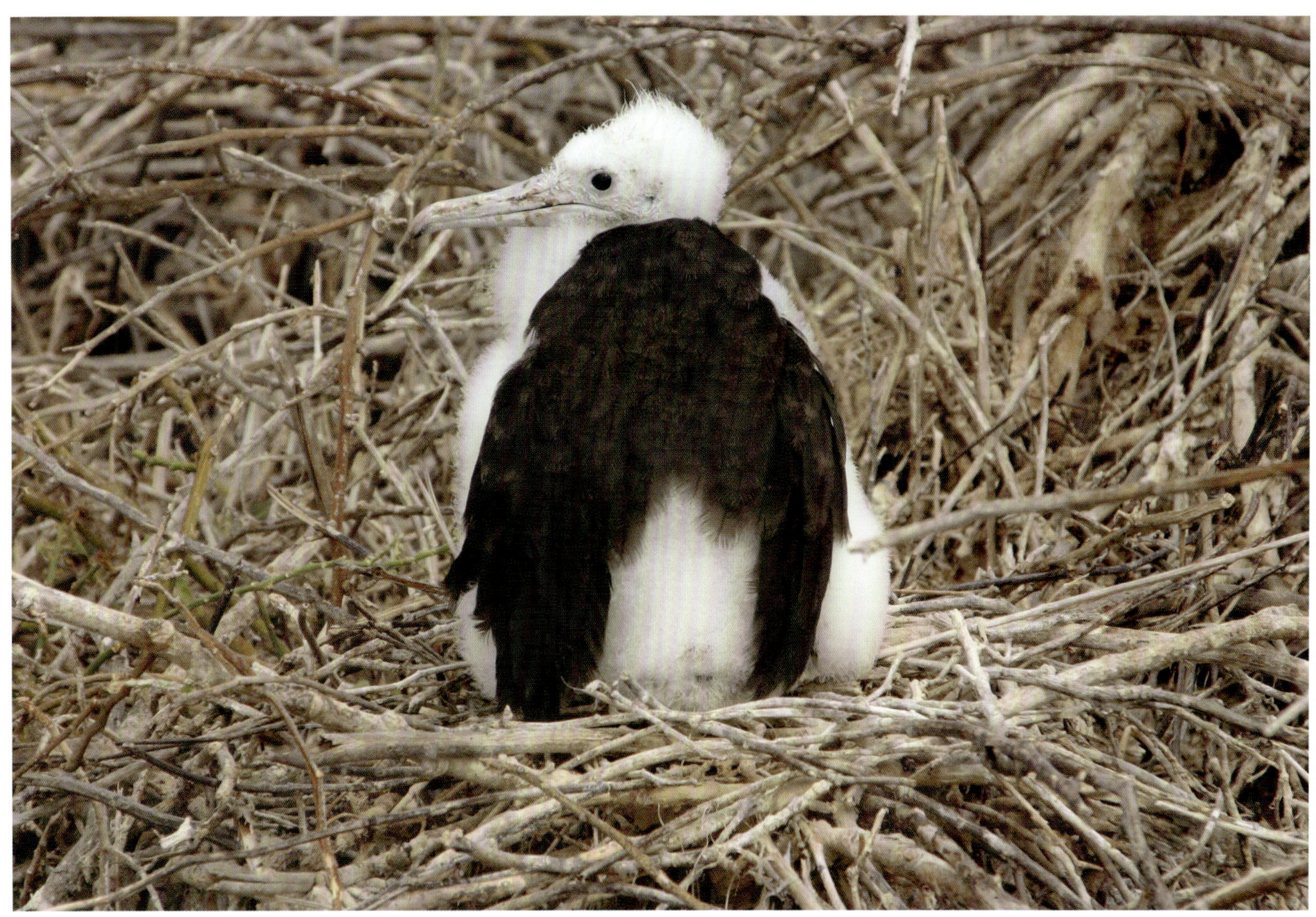

The juvenile Great Frigatebird sits on his nest.

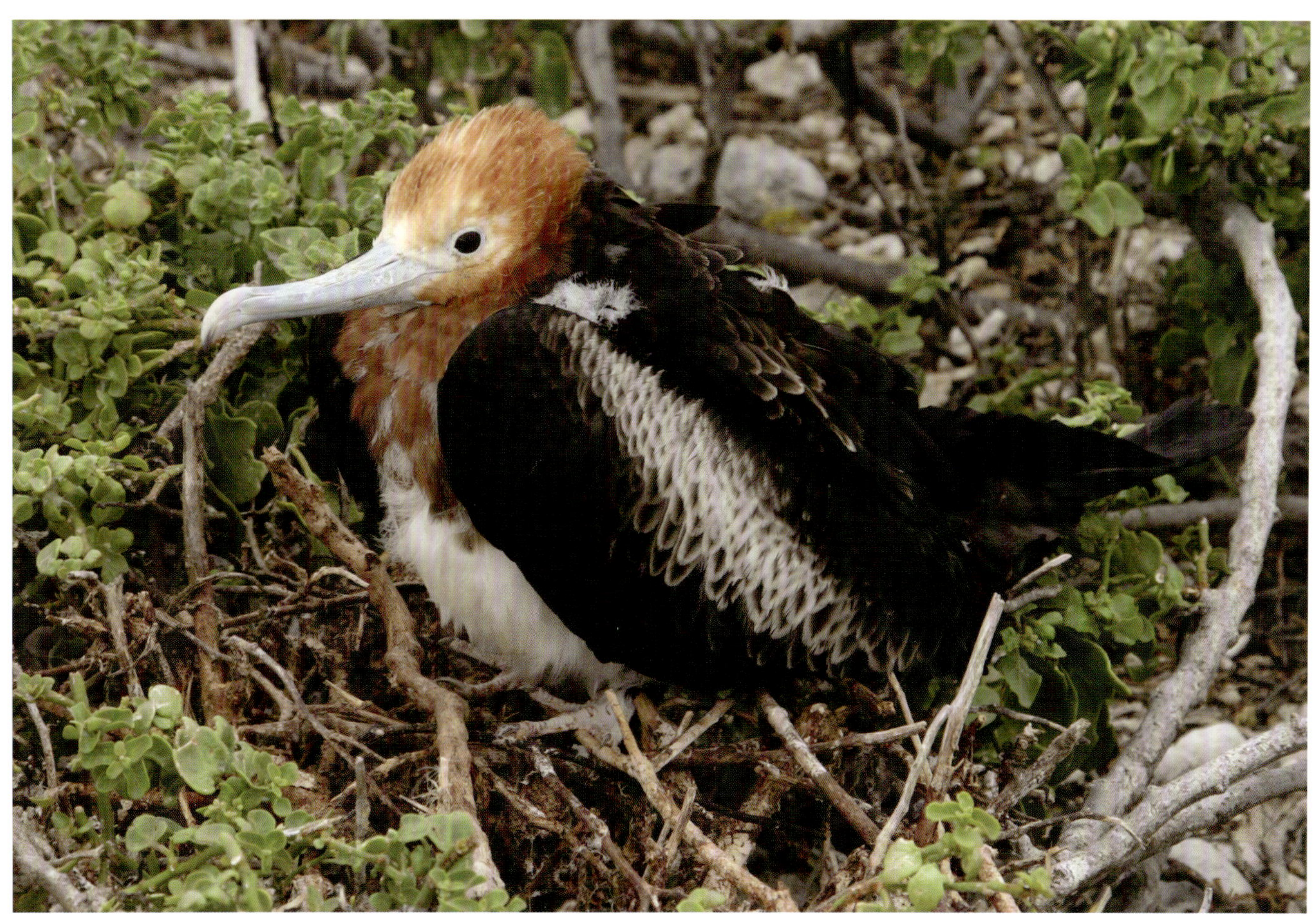

He has orange feathers and a long beak.

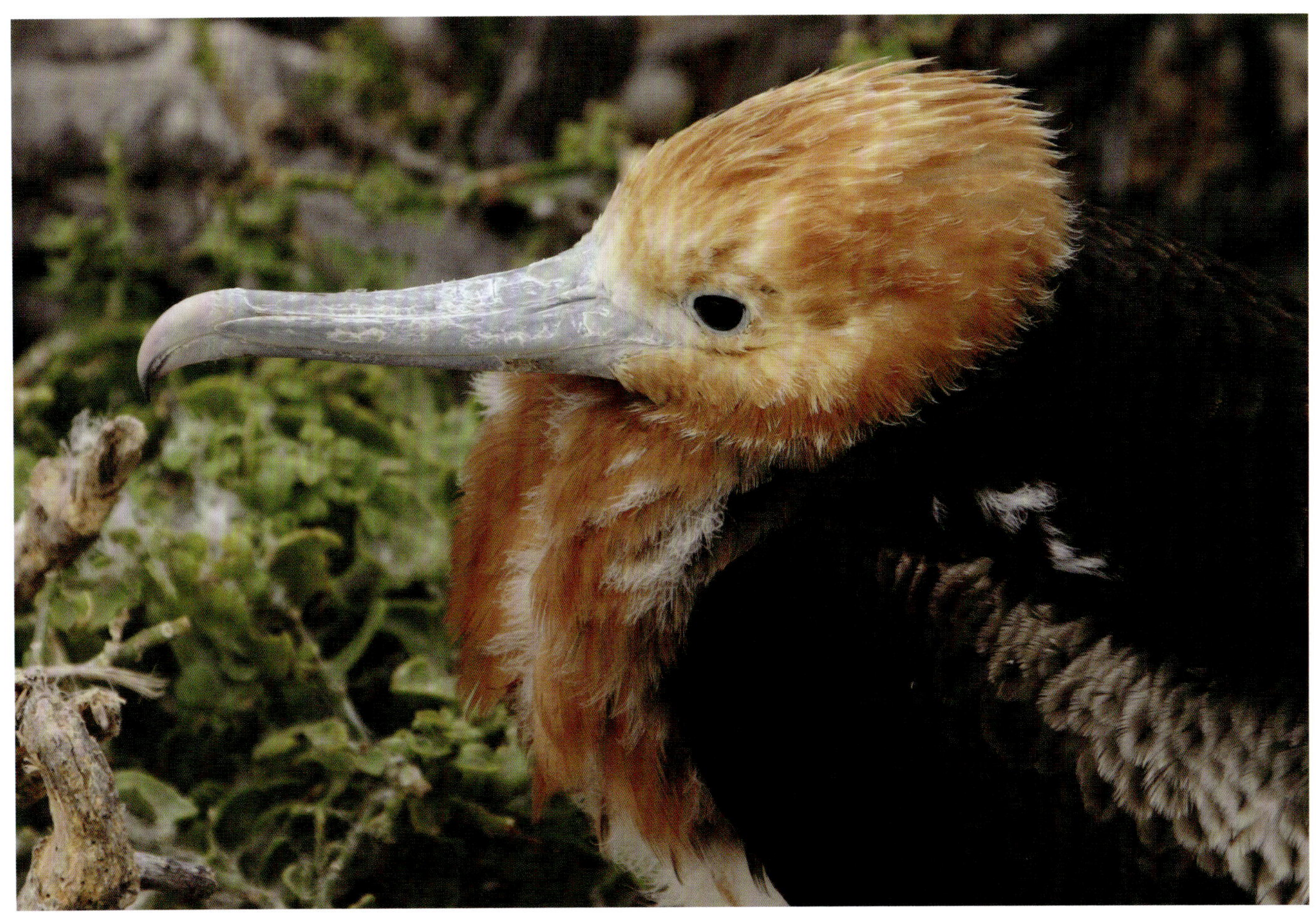

The Swallow-tailed Gull stands alone on the beach.

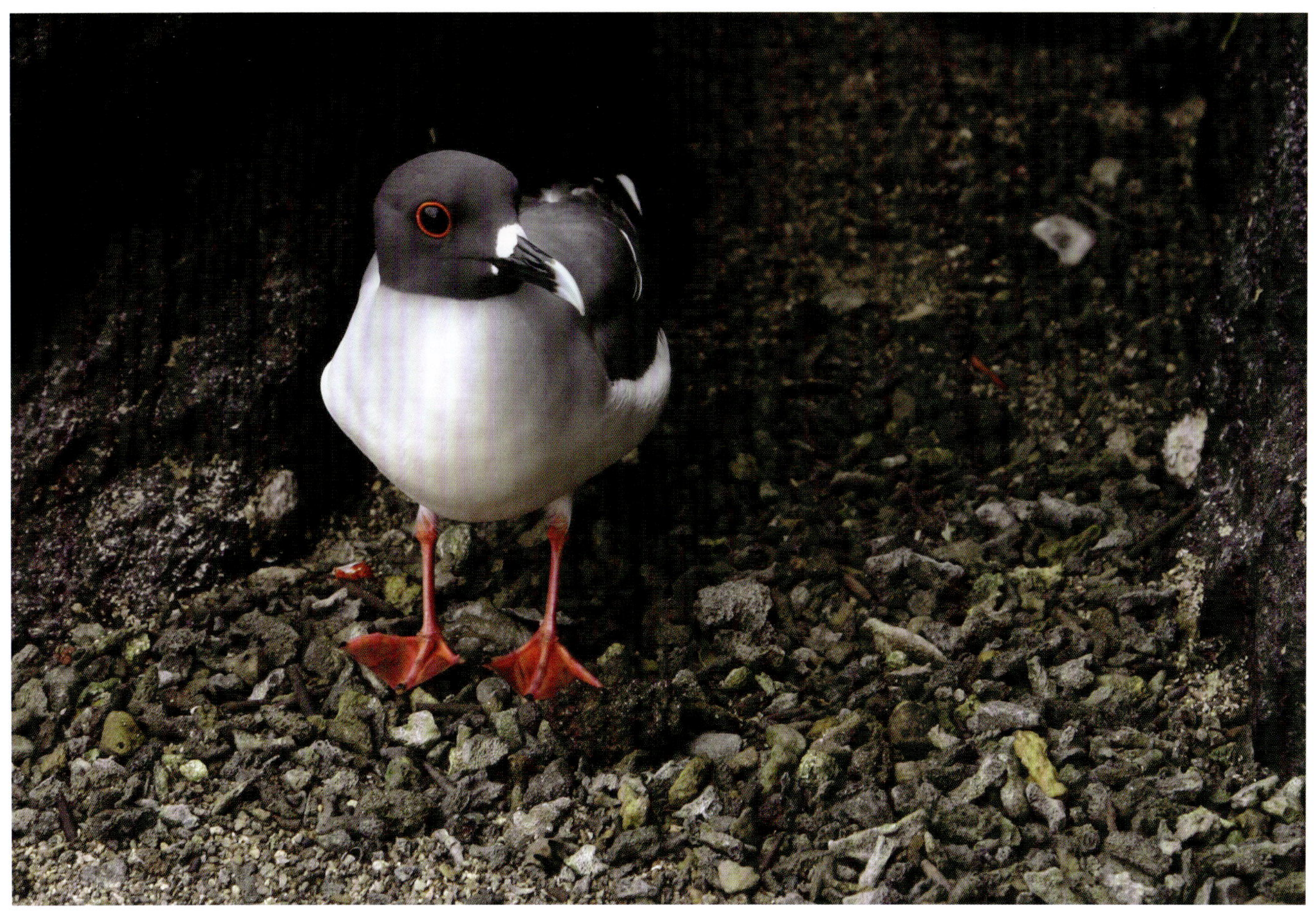

He finds a mate nearby.

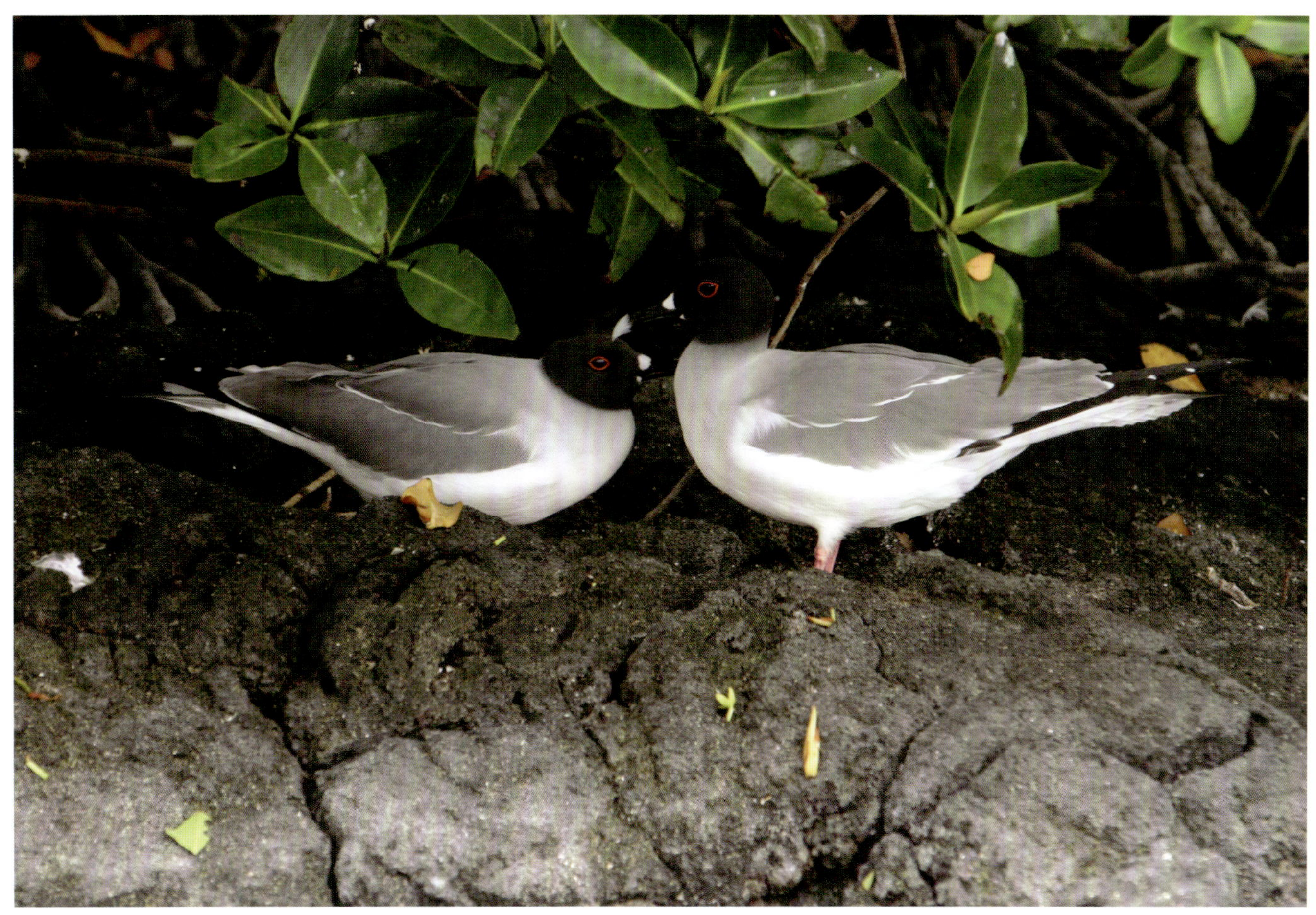

The Swallow-tailed Gulls make their nest in the rocks.

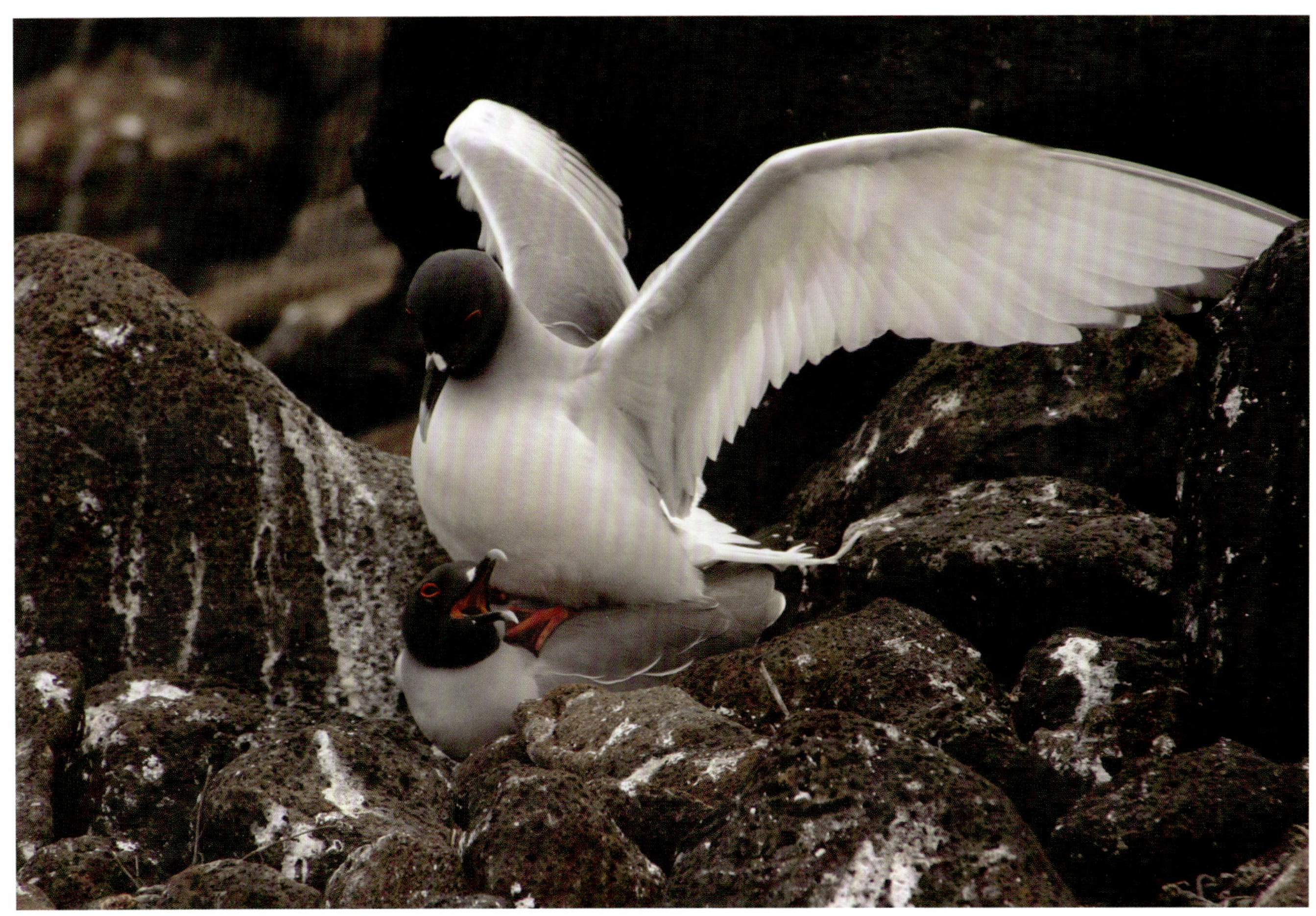

The juvenile Swallow-tailed Gull does not look like his parents at all.

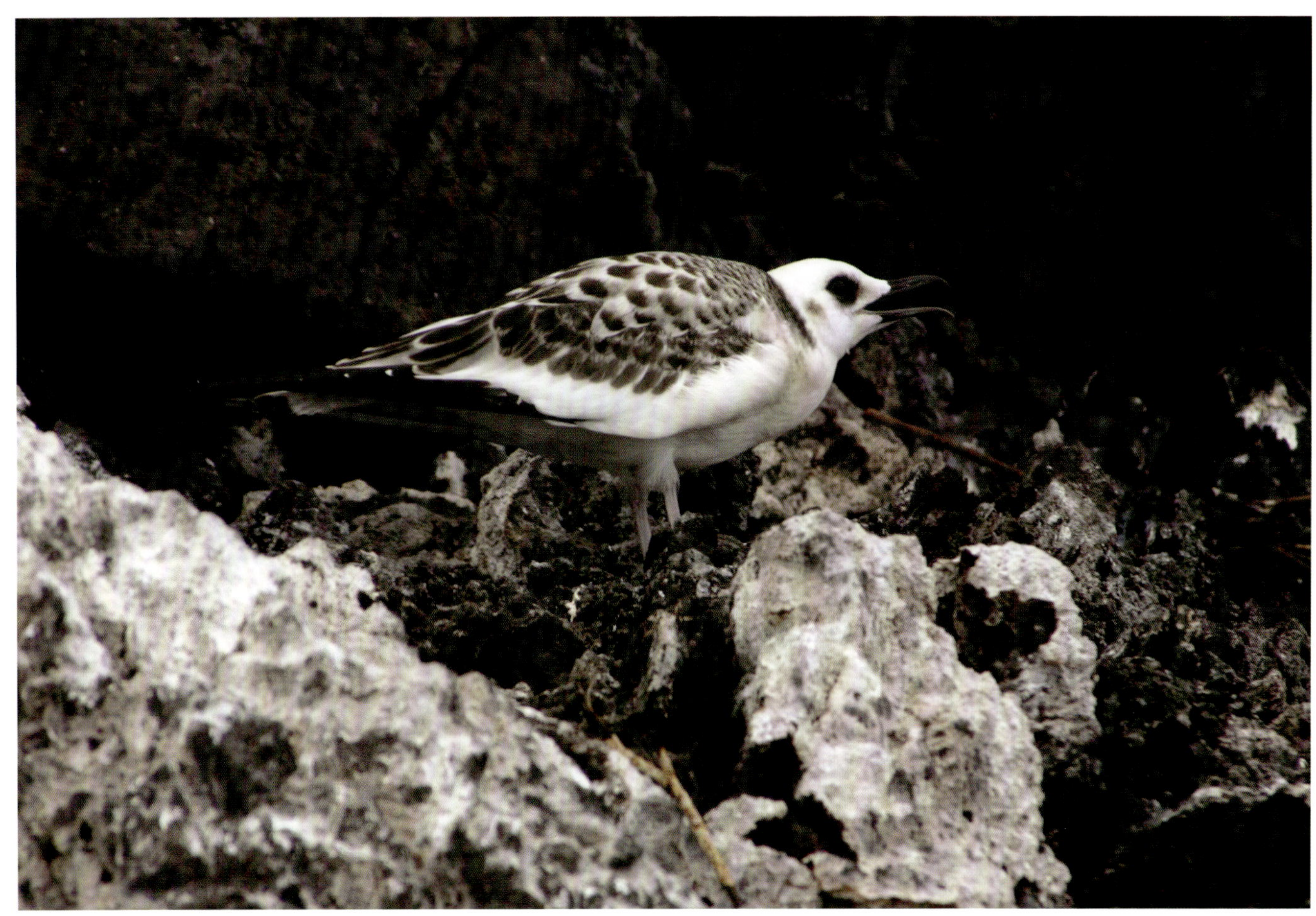

But soon, he will.

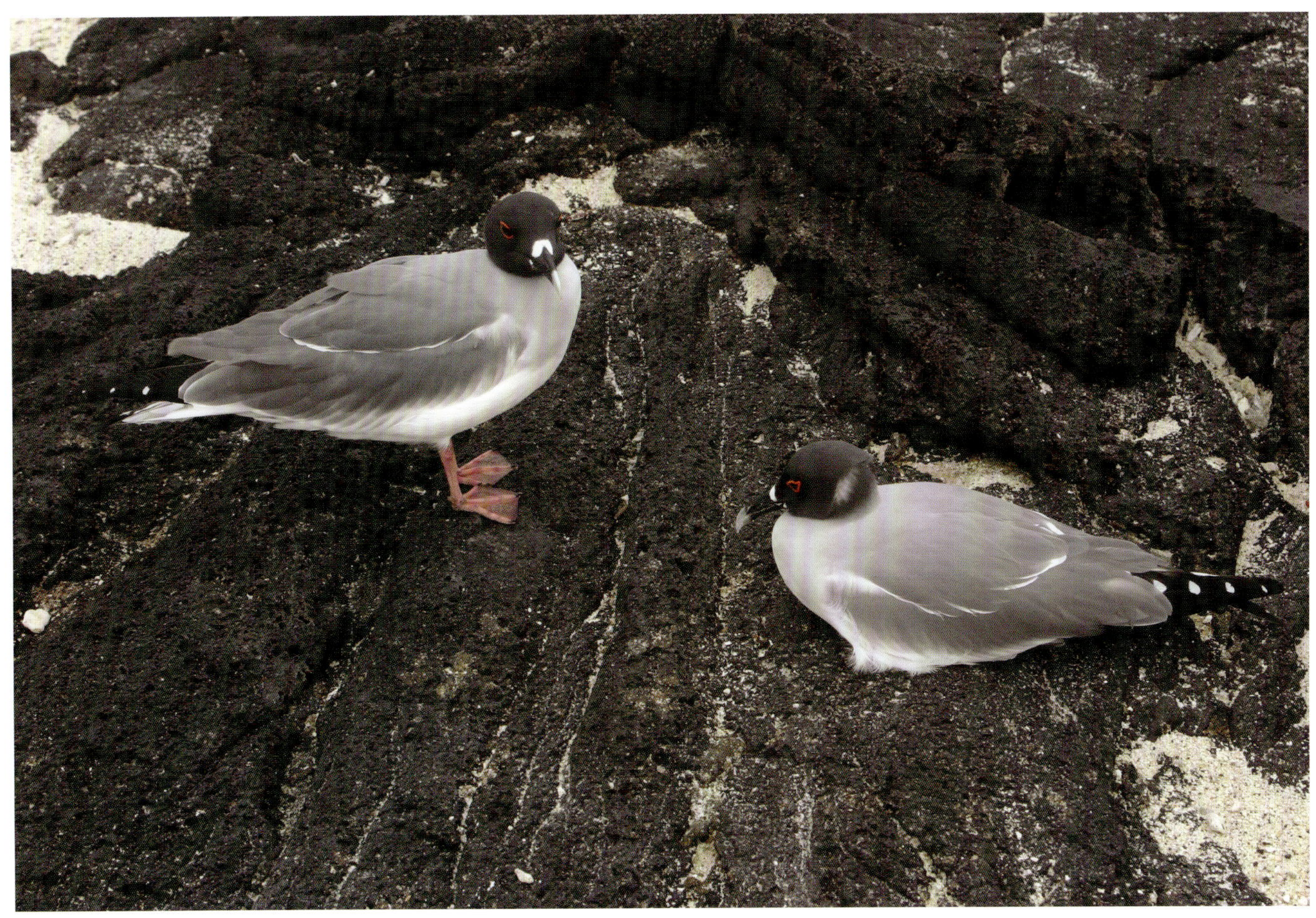

The American Flamingos stand in a lagoon.

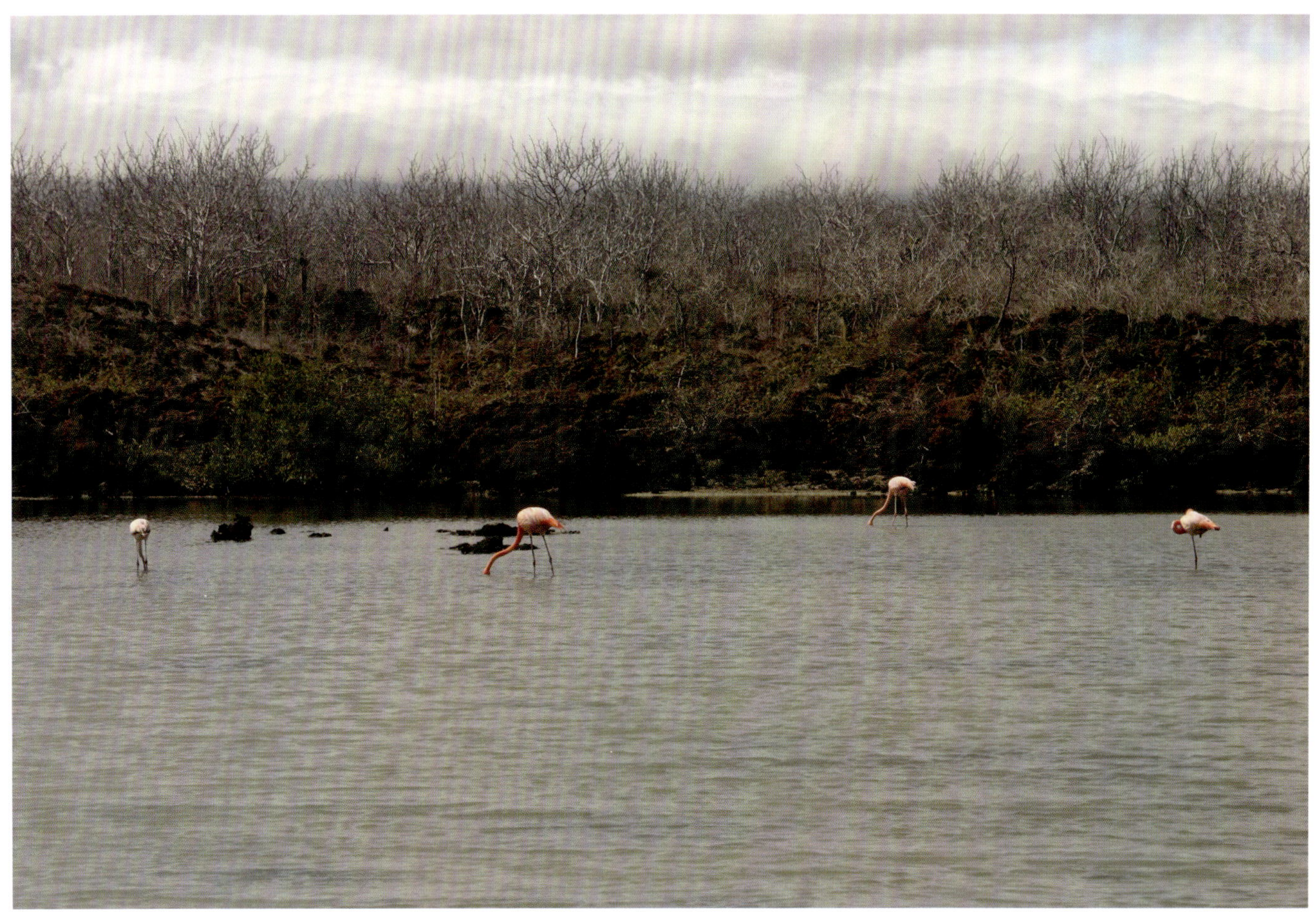

They have beautiful pink feathers.

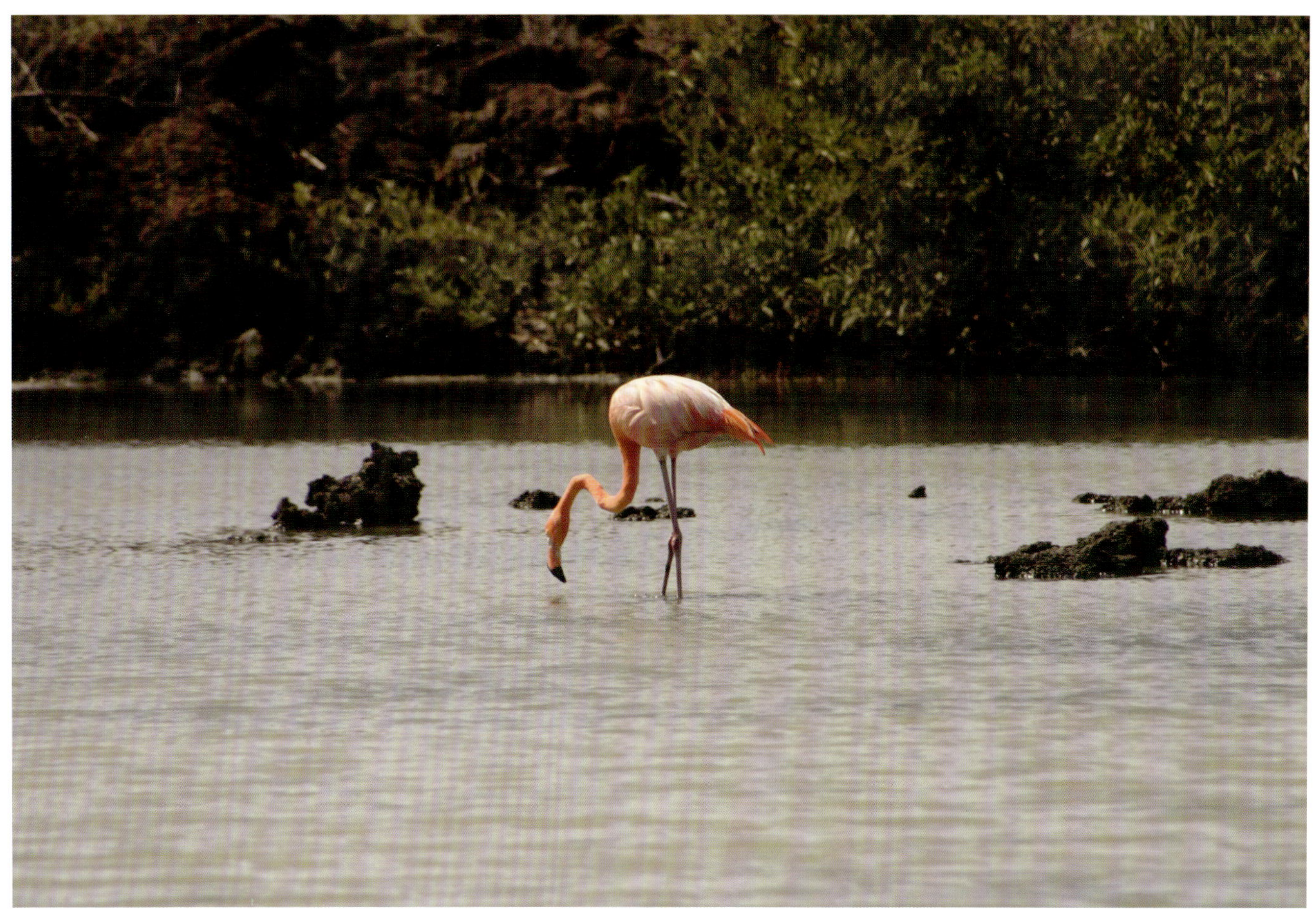

The Vegetarian Finch eats one yellow flower.

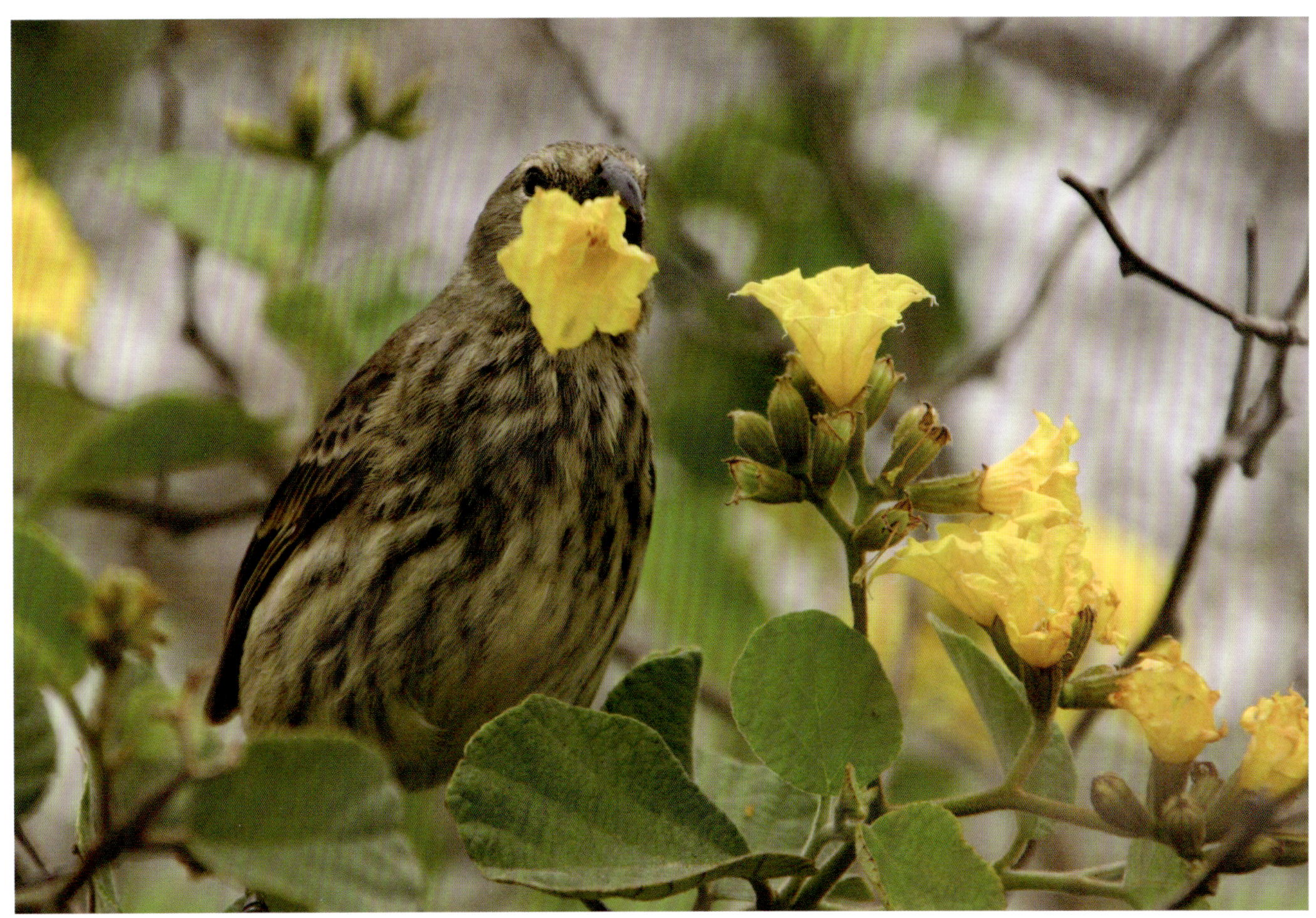

And then another.

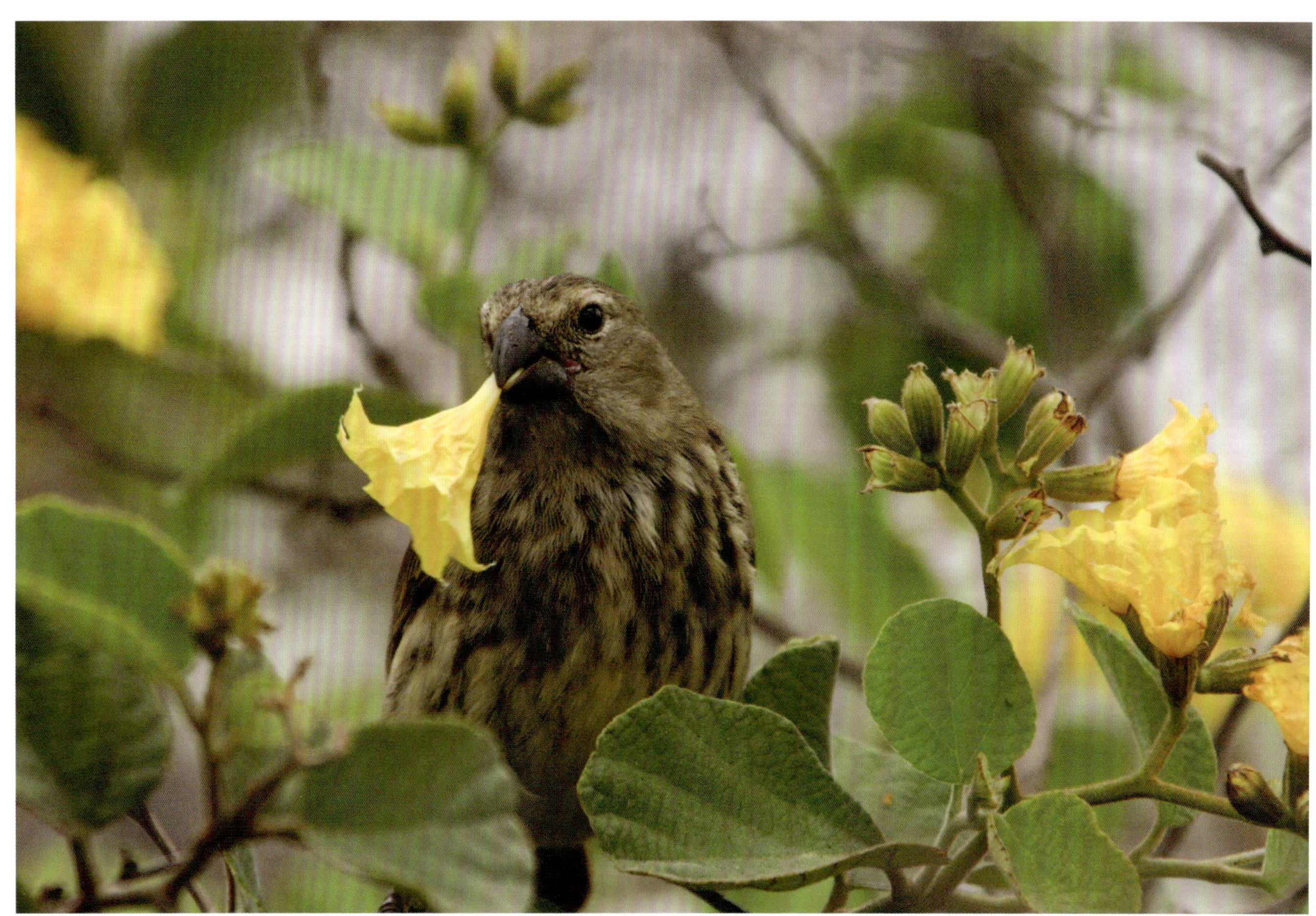

This Galapagos Mockingbird perches on a stem.

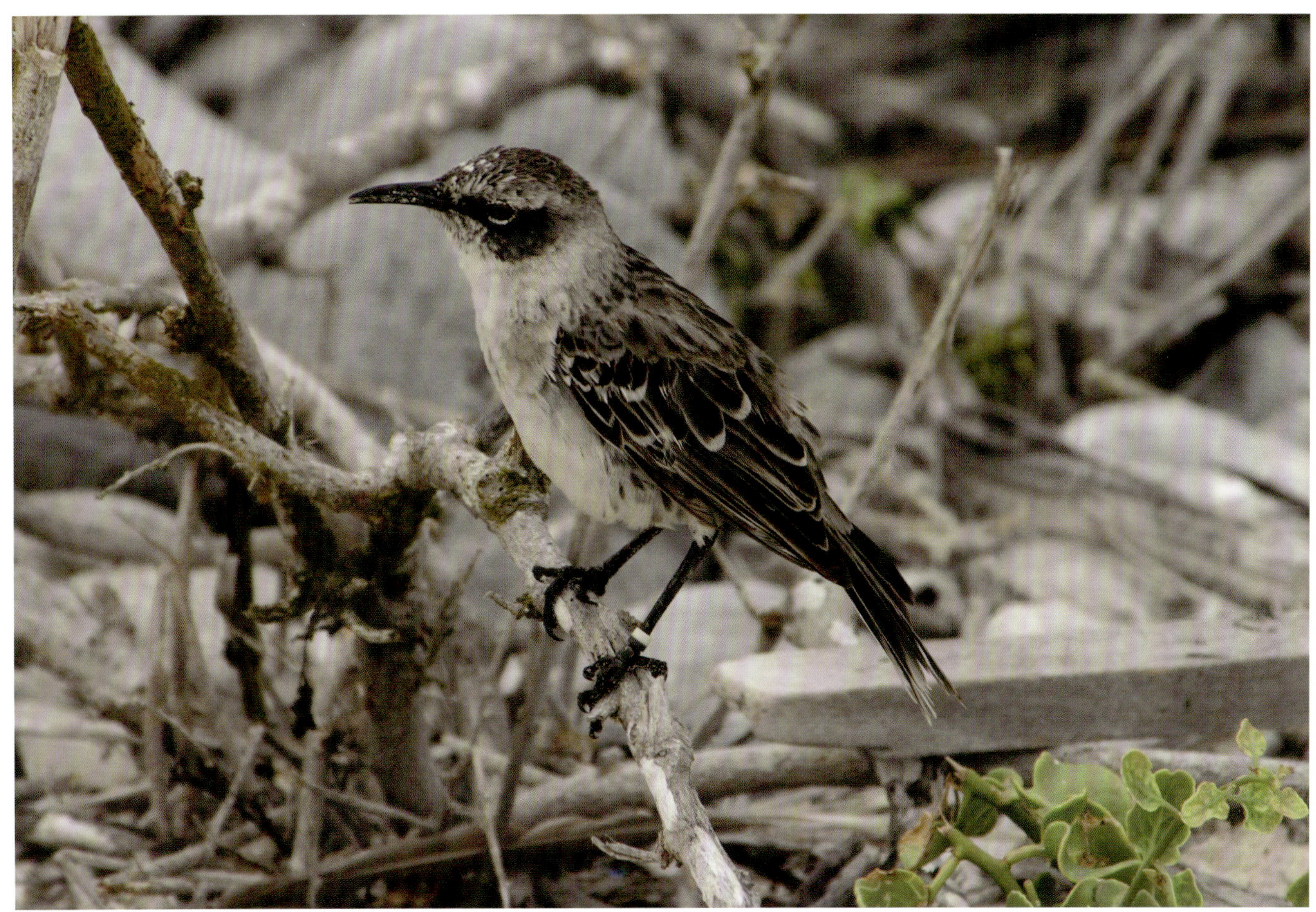

And this one takes a ride on a Galapagos Giant Tortoise.

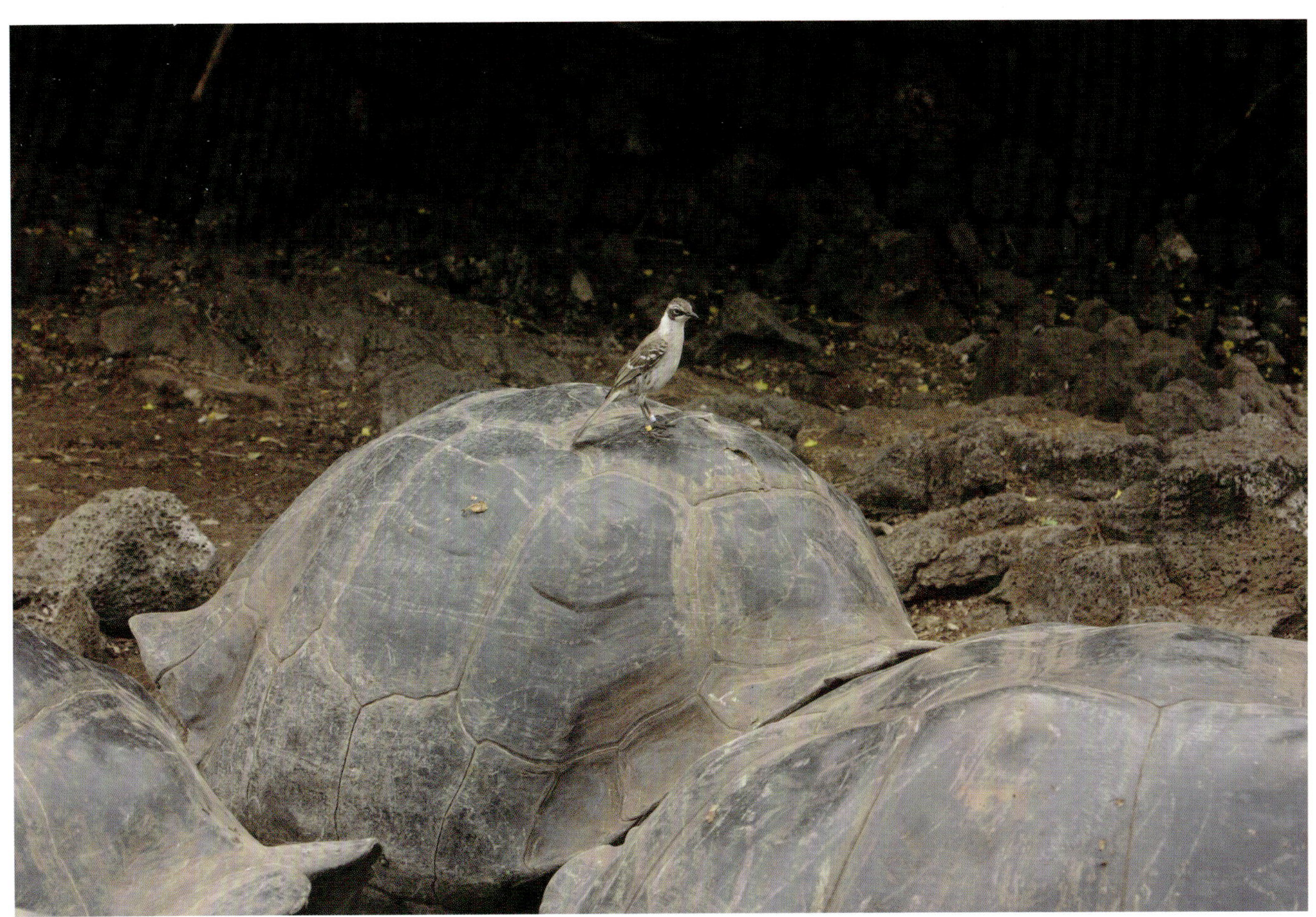

As does the Yellow Warbler.

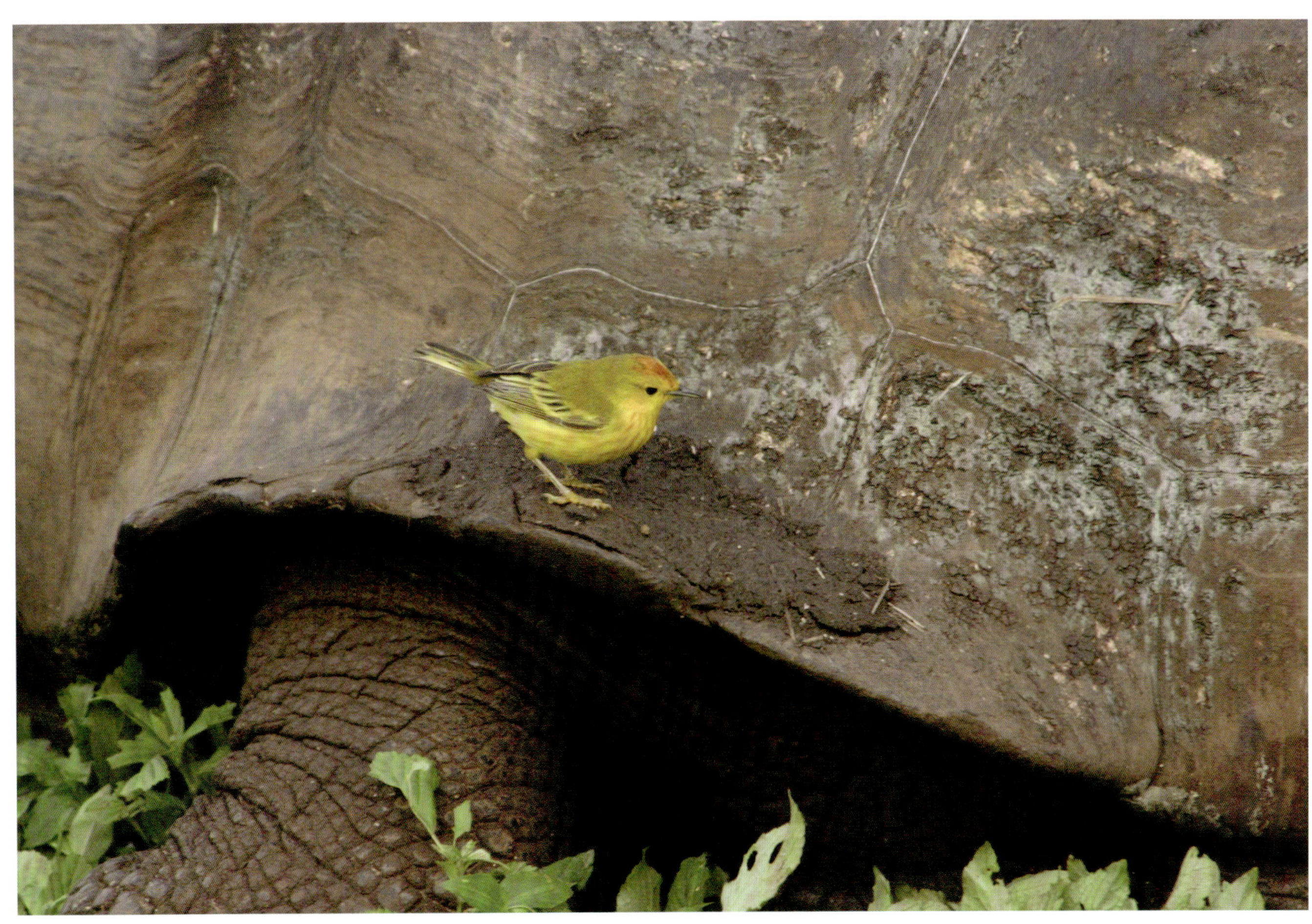

The adult Lava Heron waits patiently.

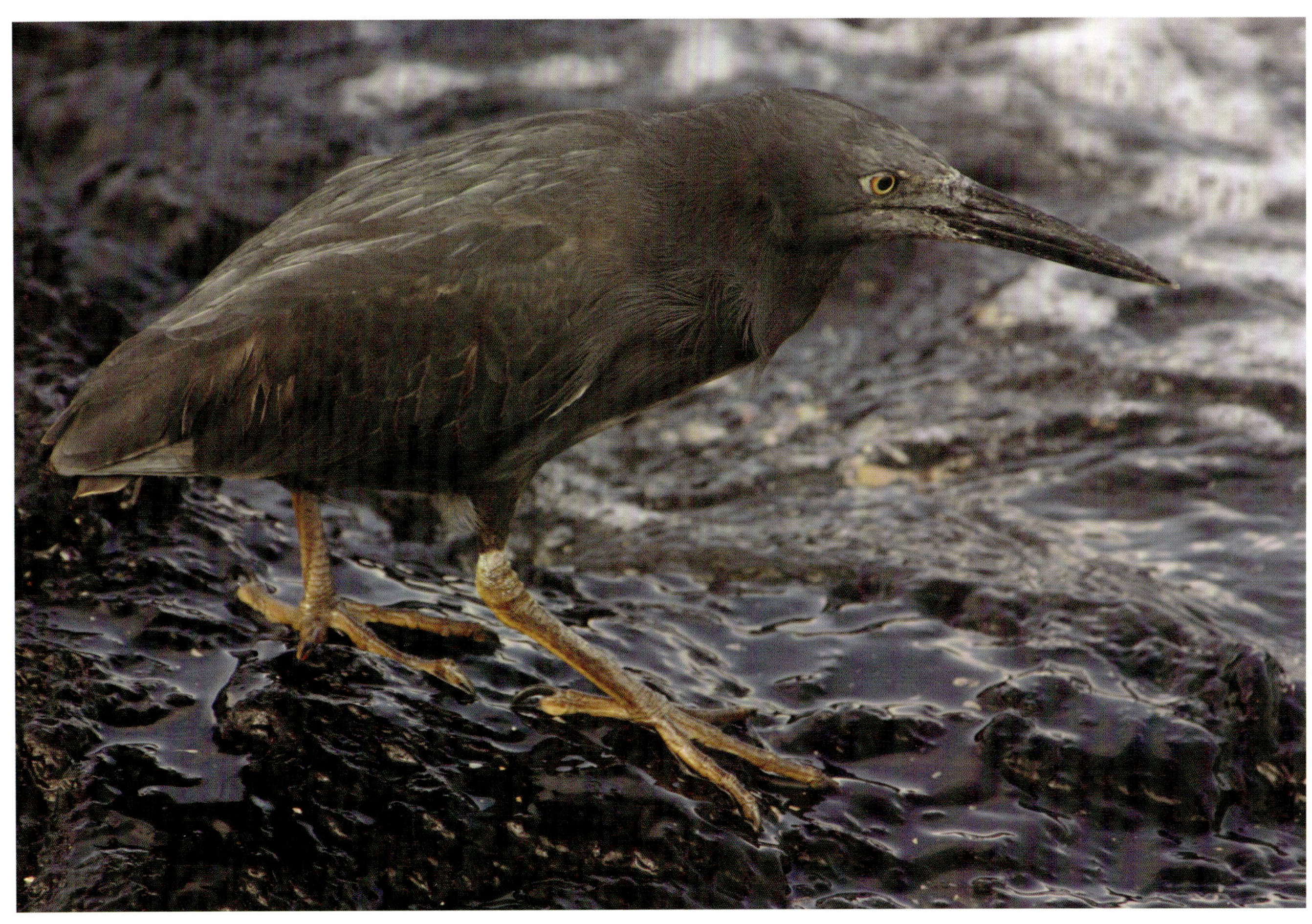

And then pokes his head out for some fish.

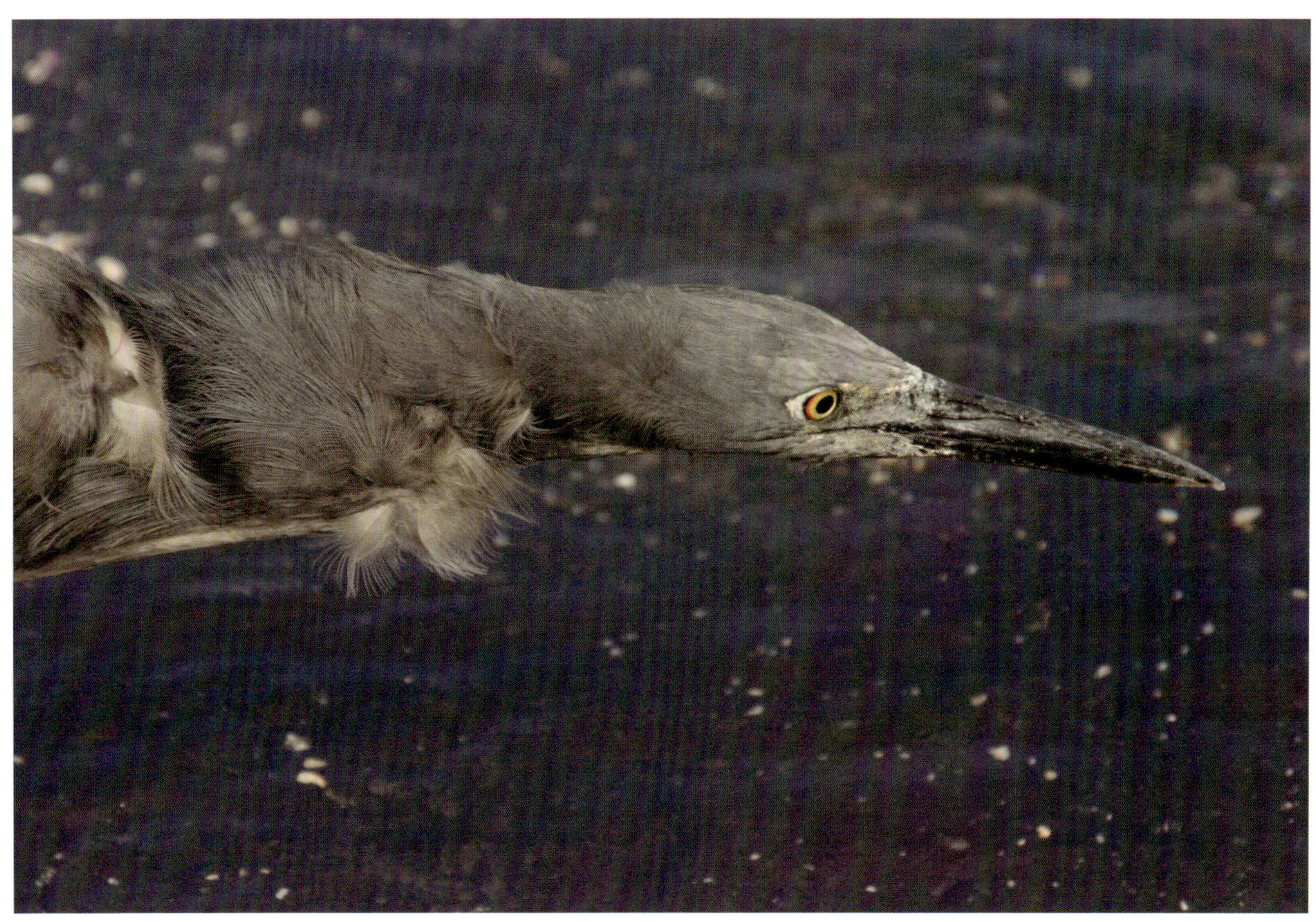

While the juvenile Lava Heron looks on.

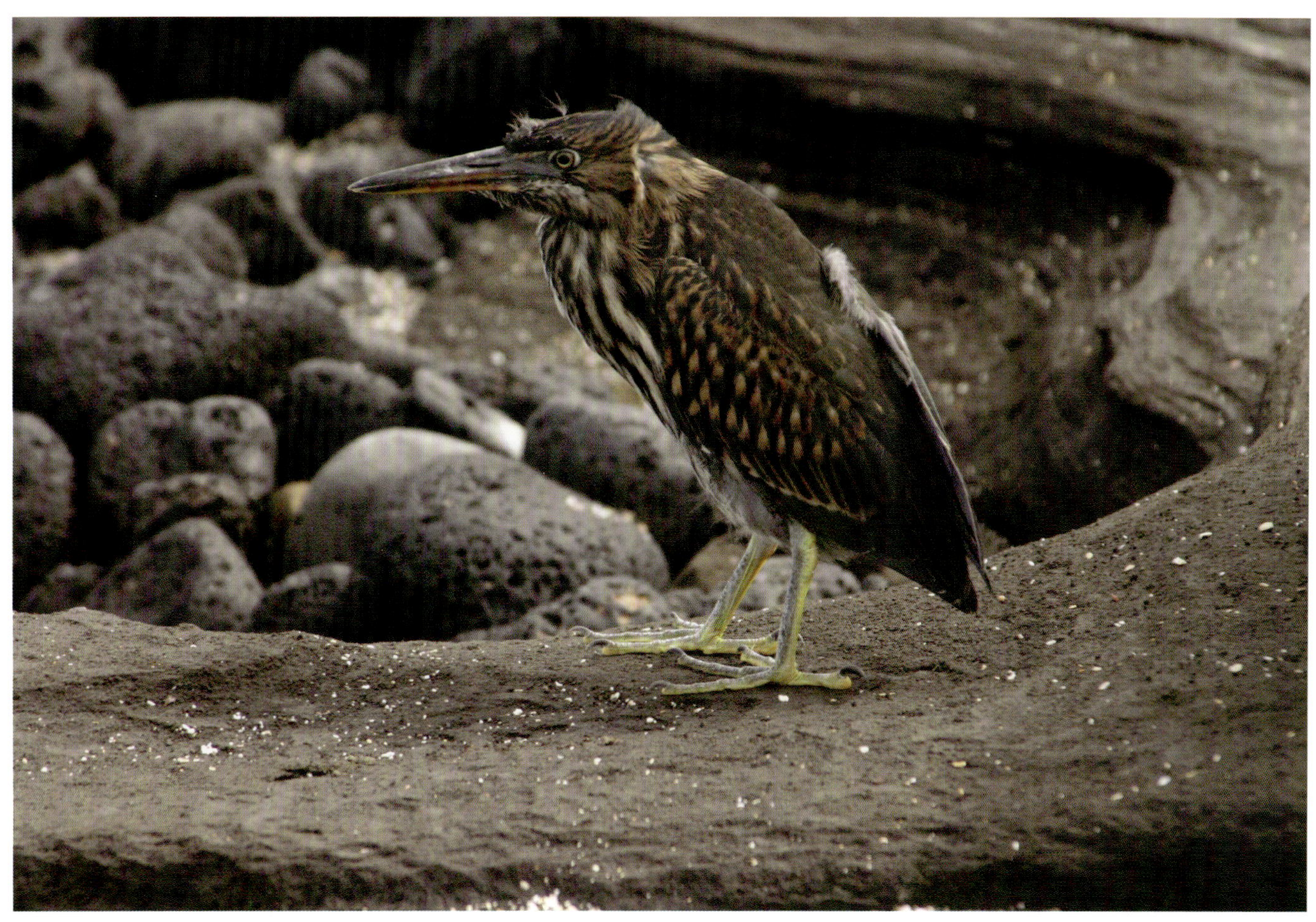

As does the Yellow-crowned Night-Heron.

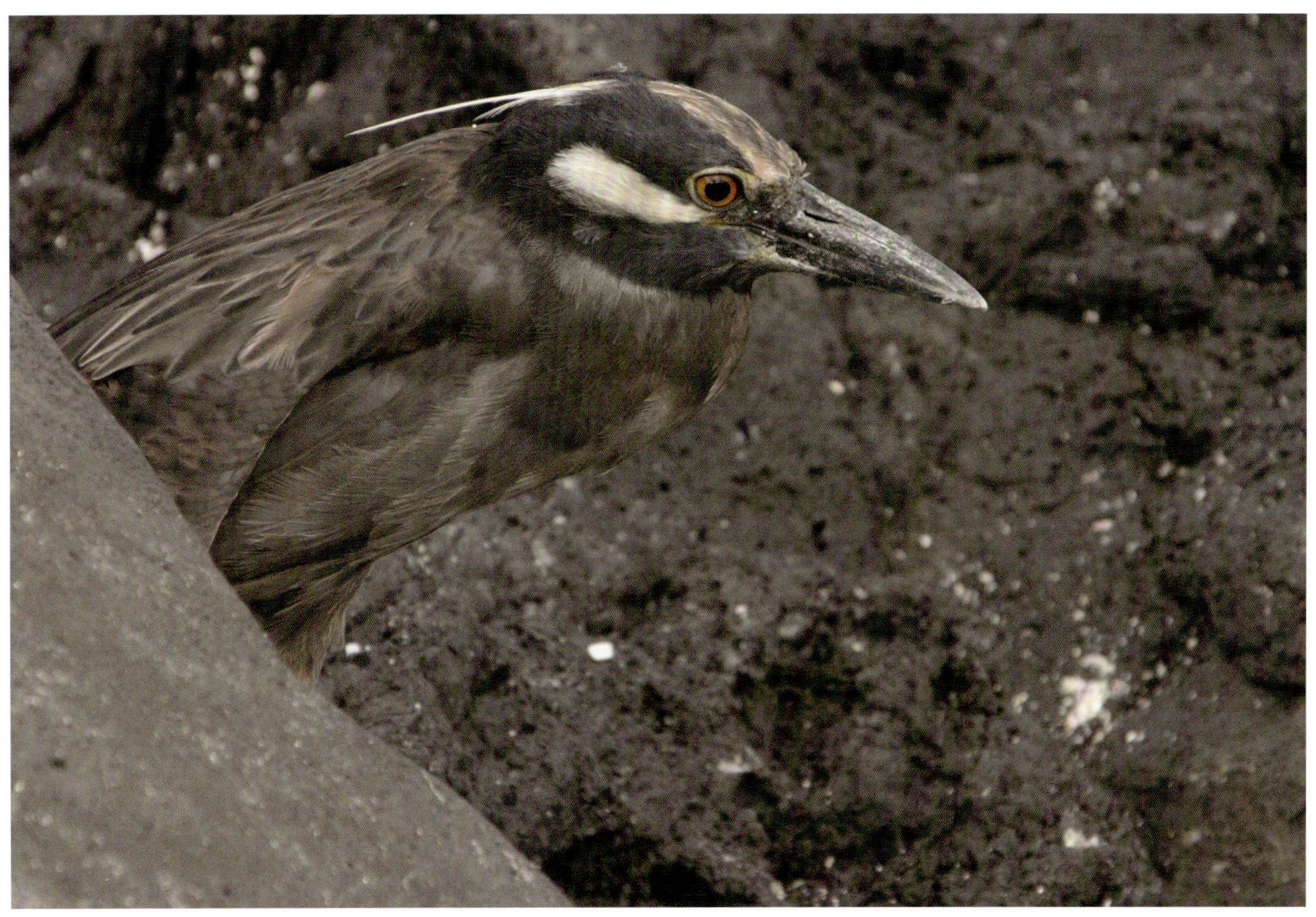

The Waved Albatrosses circle their bills.

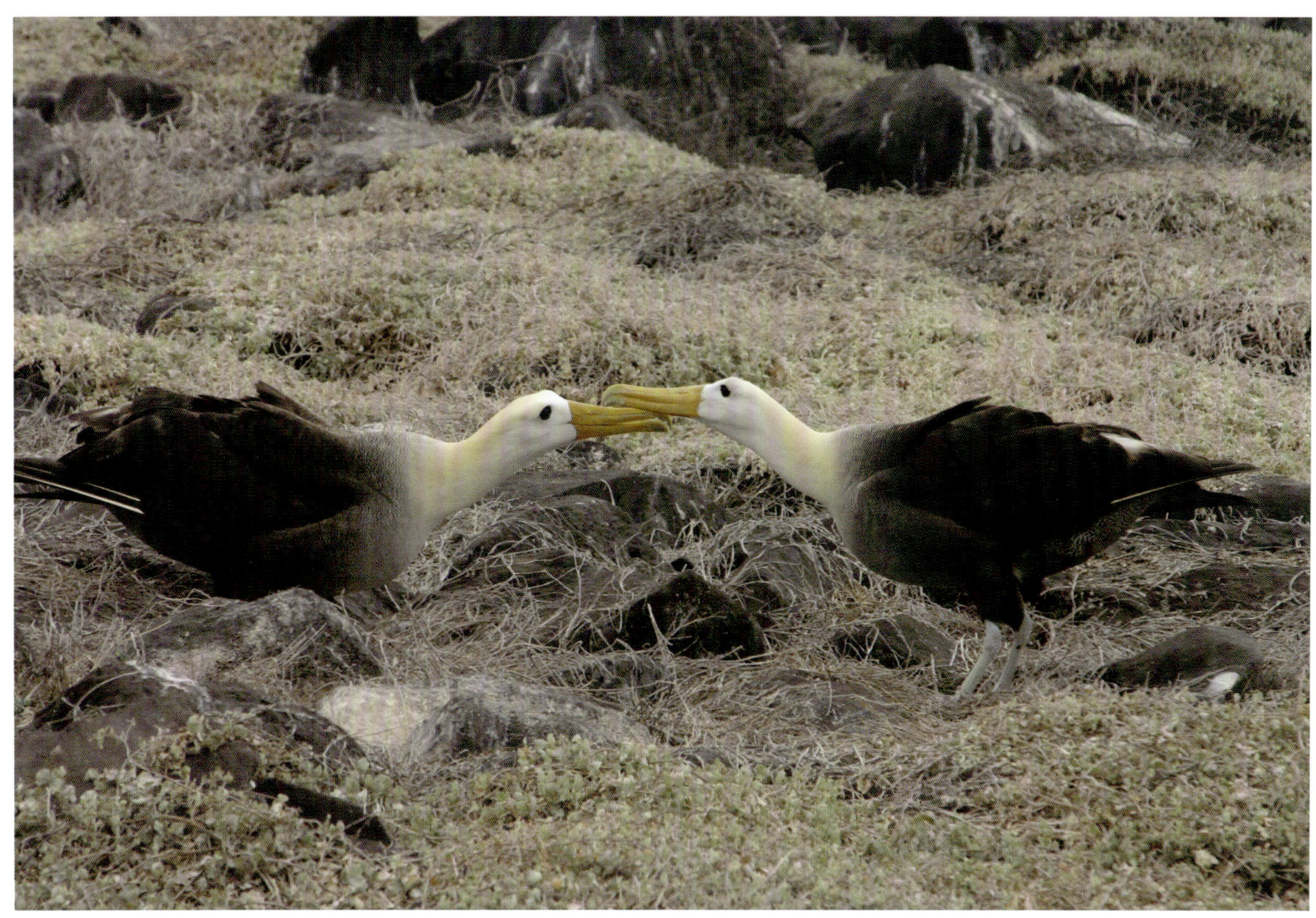

One bird opens its beak.

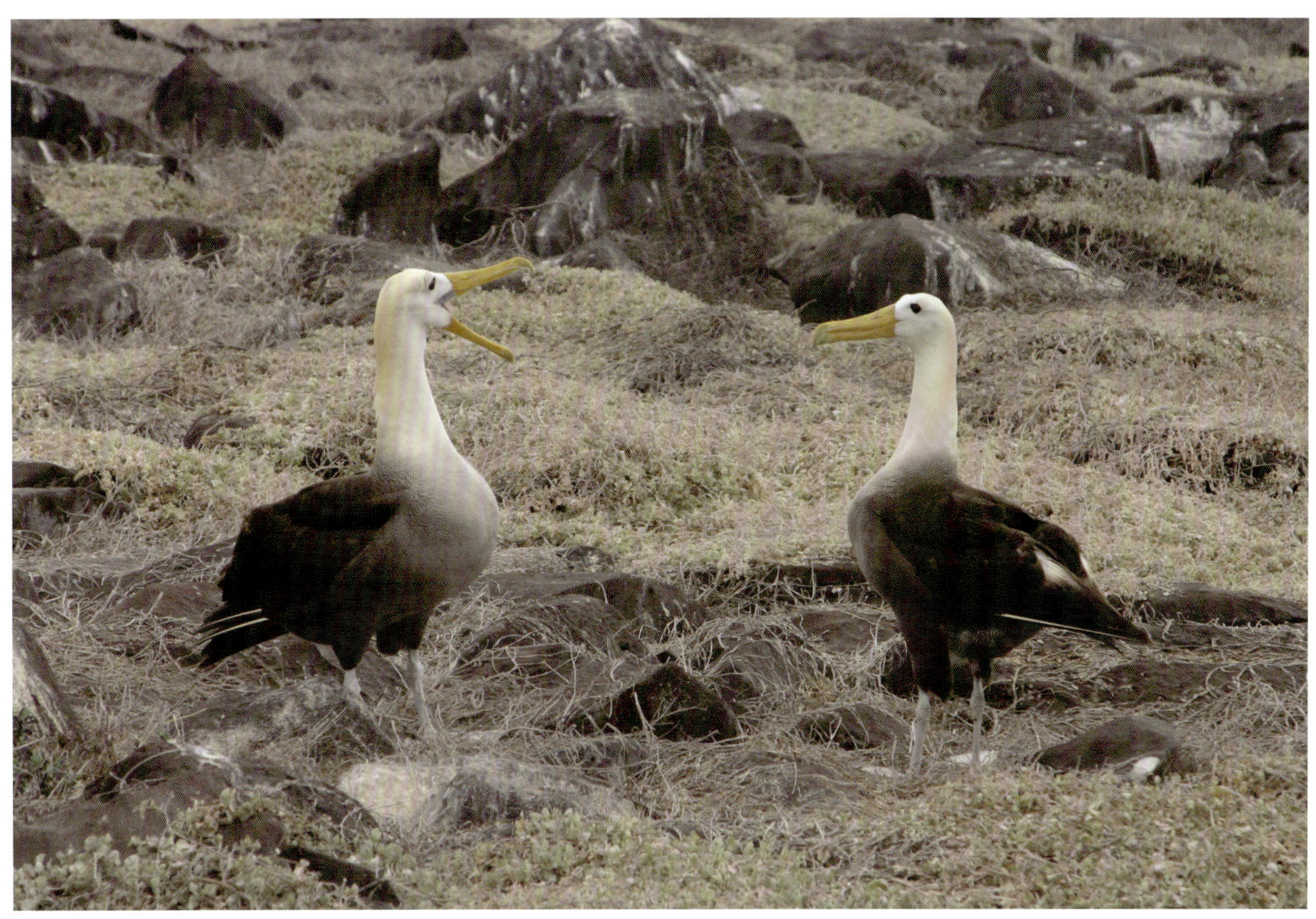

And then points to the sky.

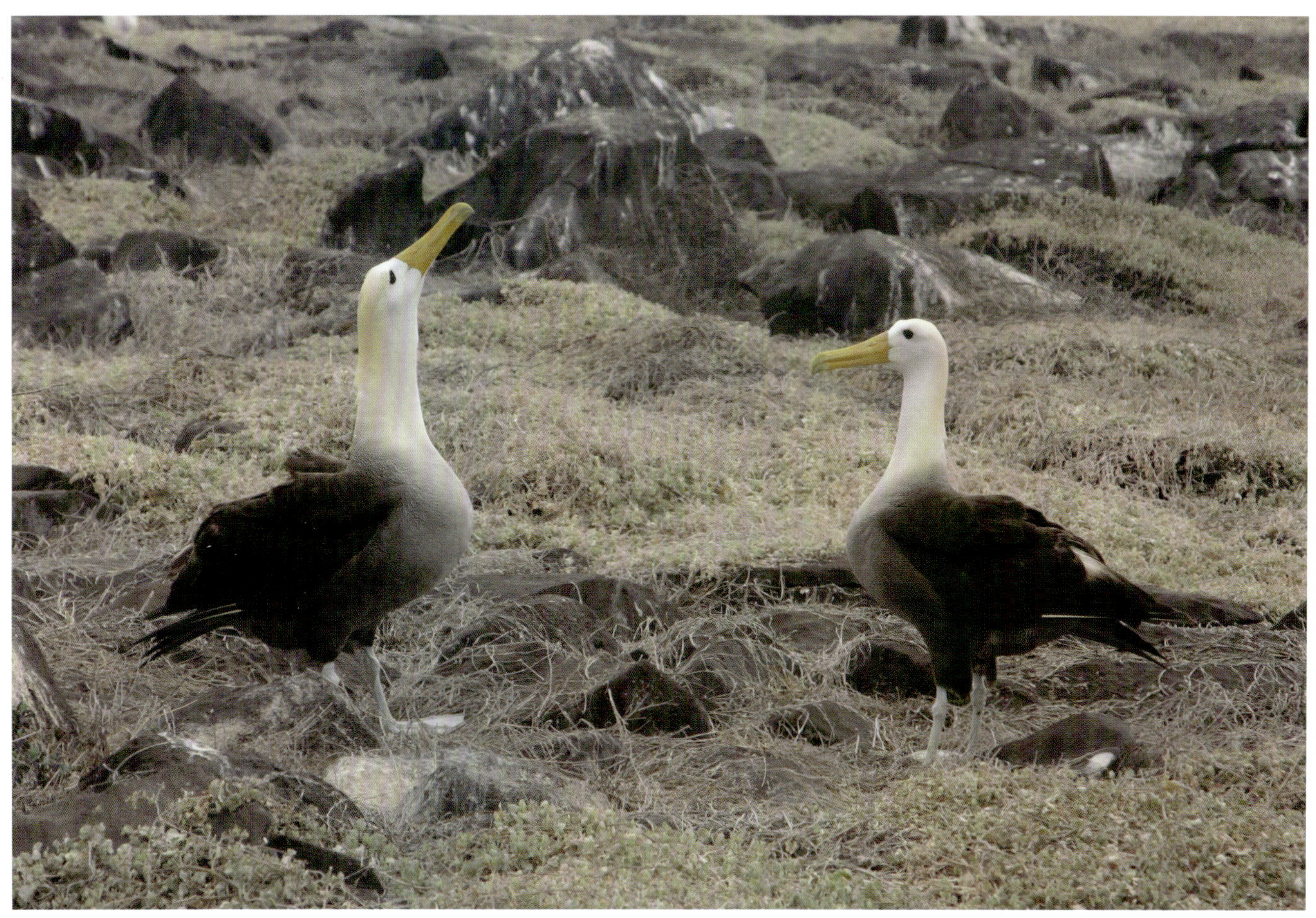

The juvenile Galapagos Hawk looks out over the bay.

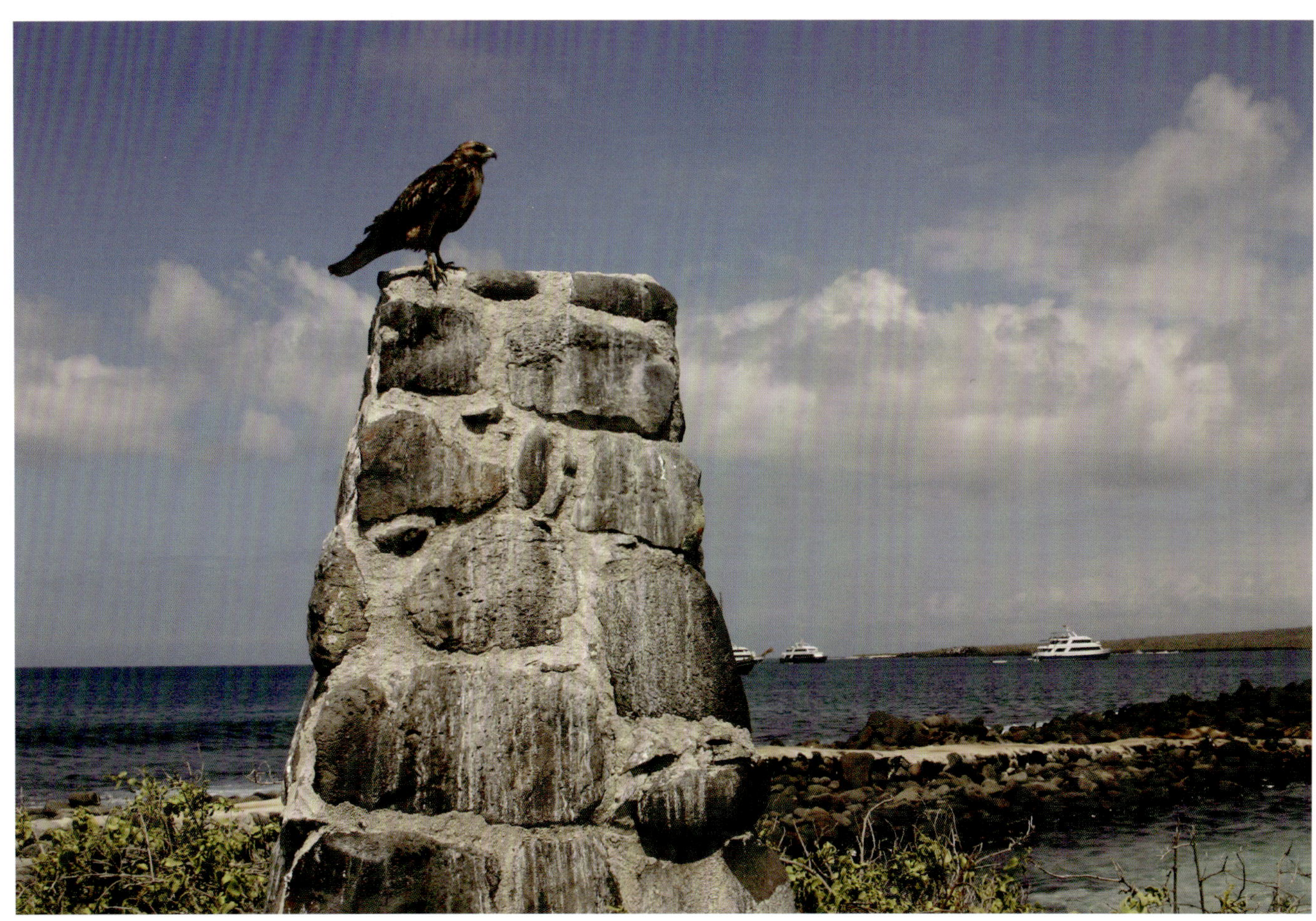

And then gets ready to fly.

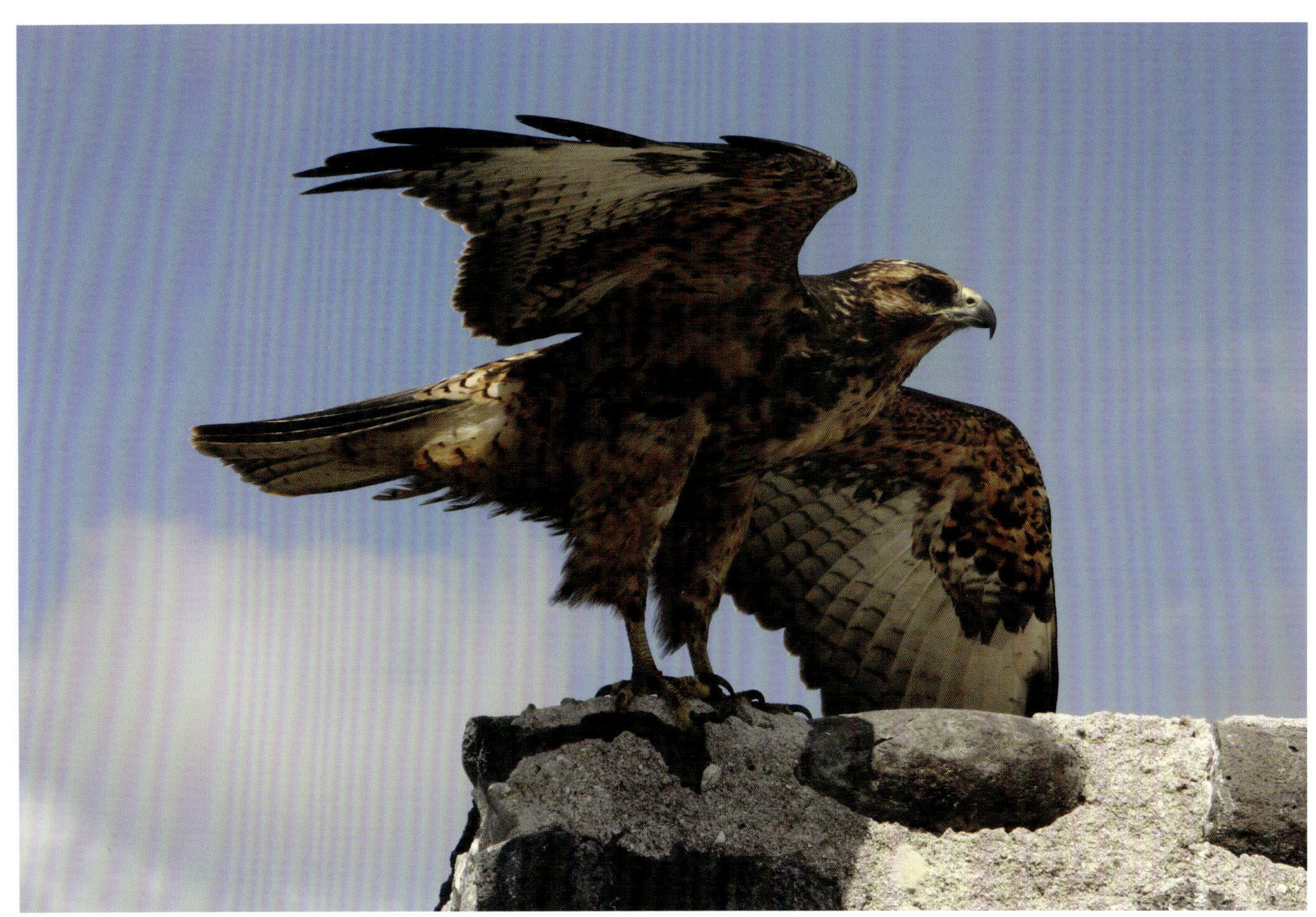

A Sanderling stands on the rocks.

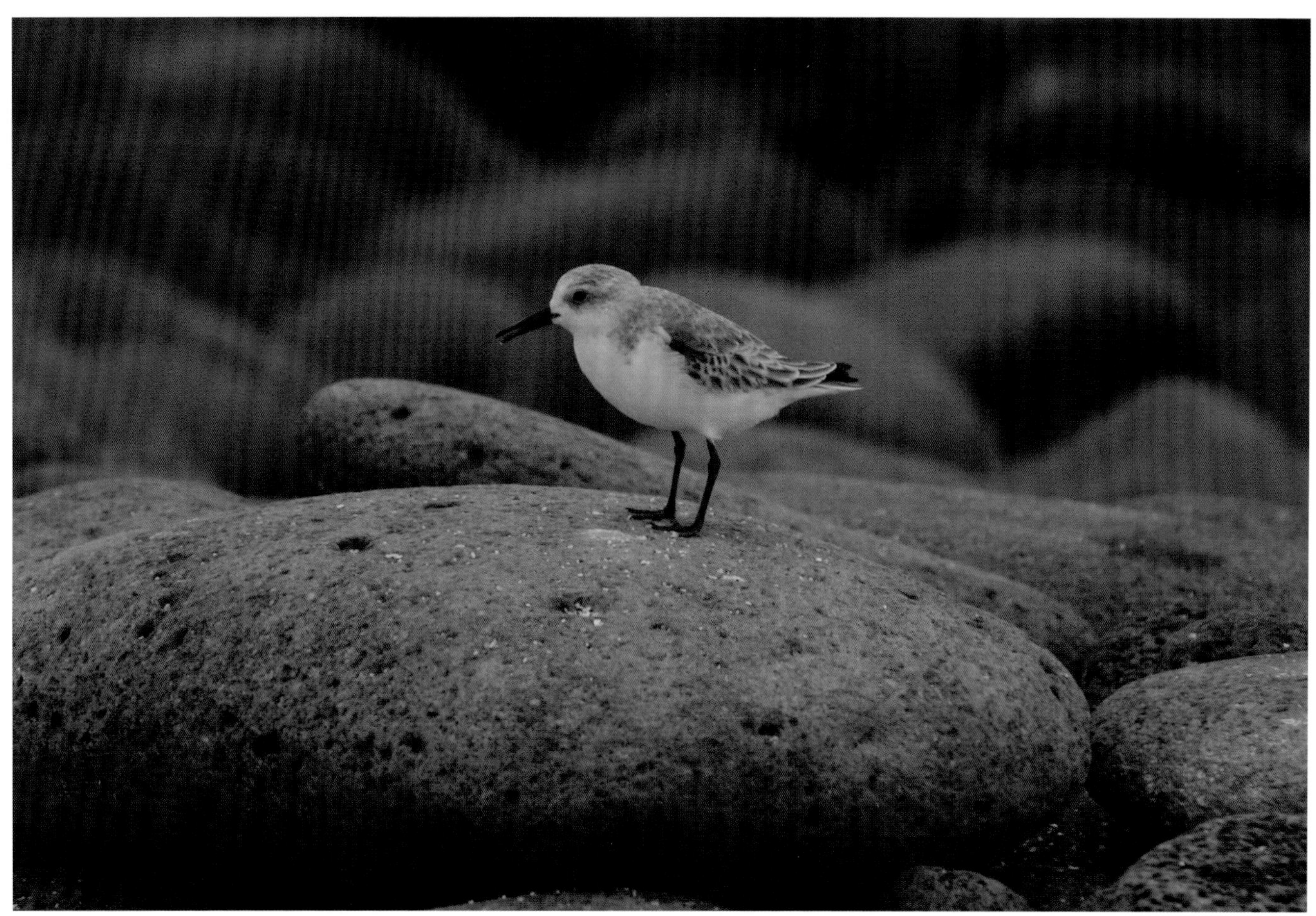

As does the Hood Mockingbird.

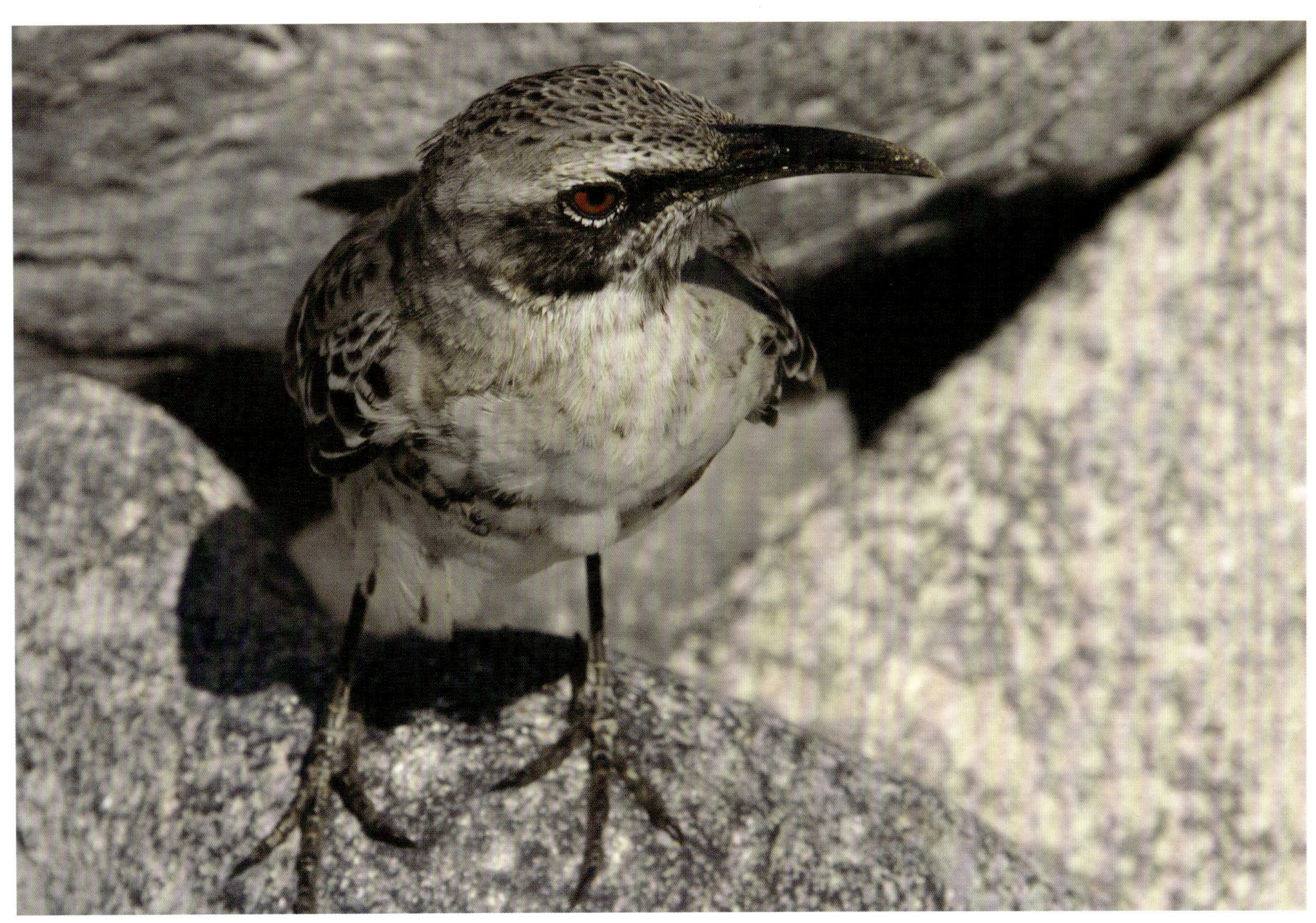

The American Oystercatcher looks for her chick.

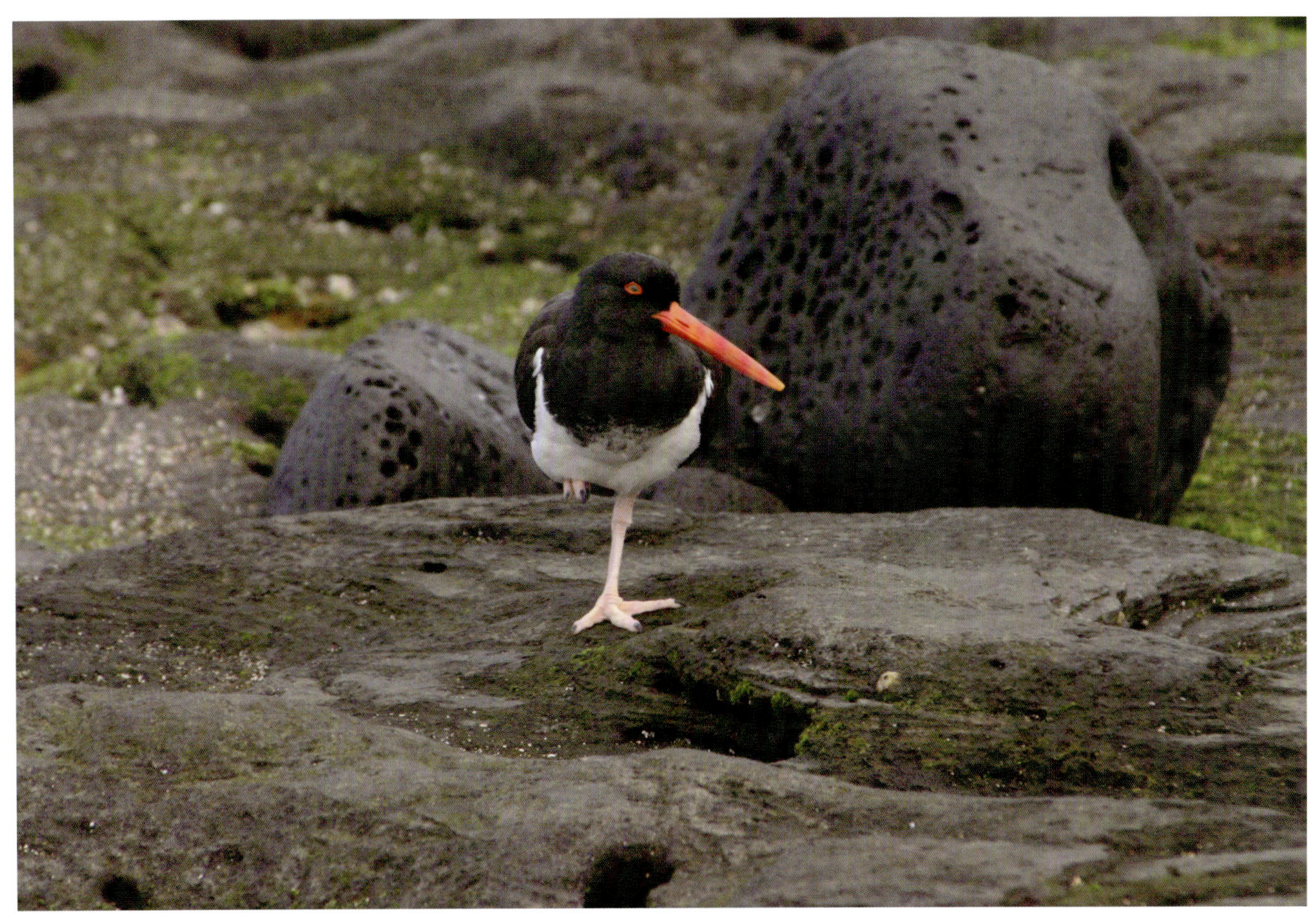

The chick is all alone.

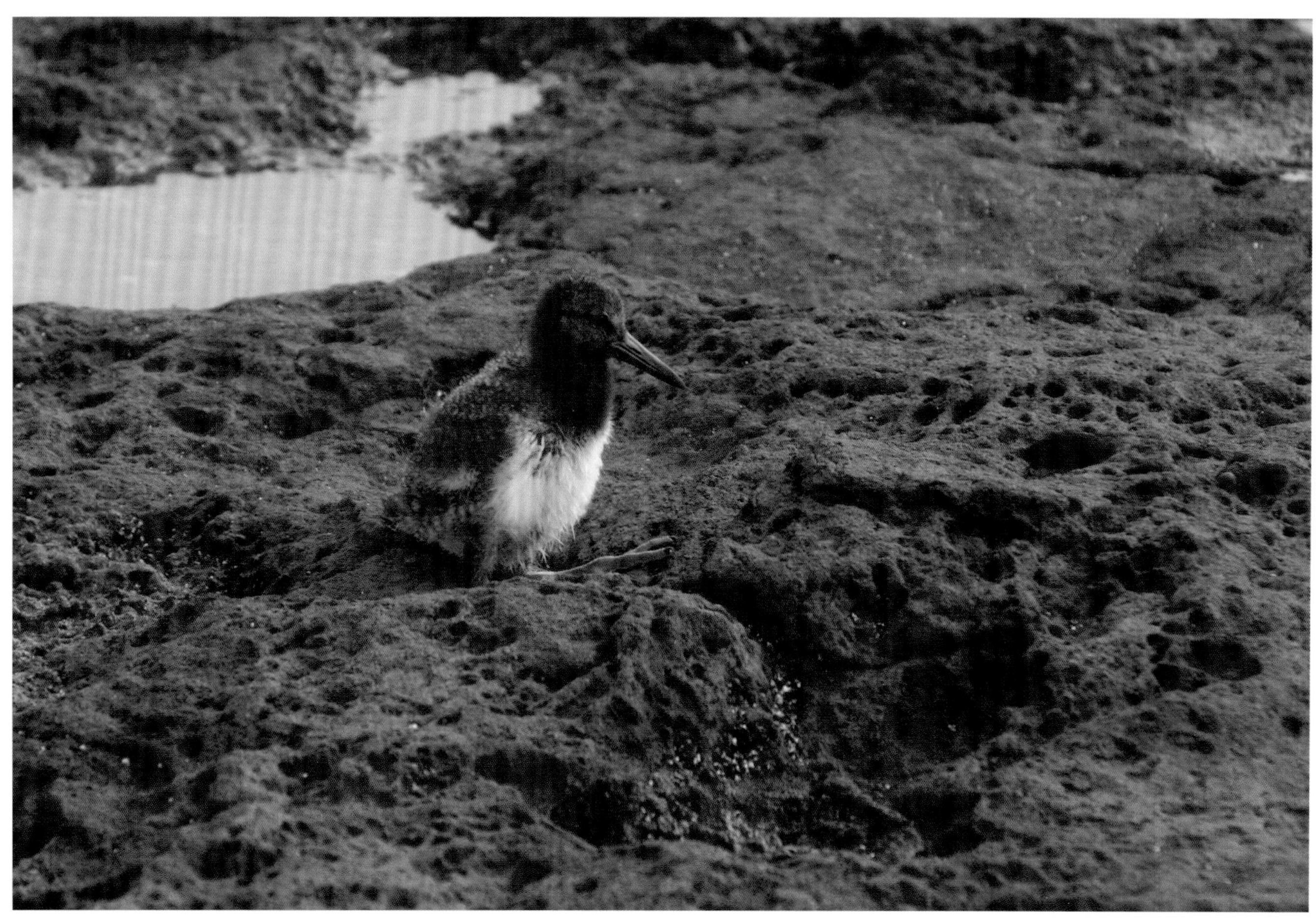

Don’t worry, Mother is here.

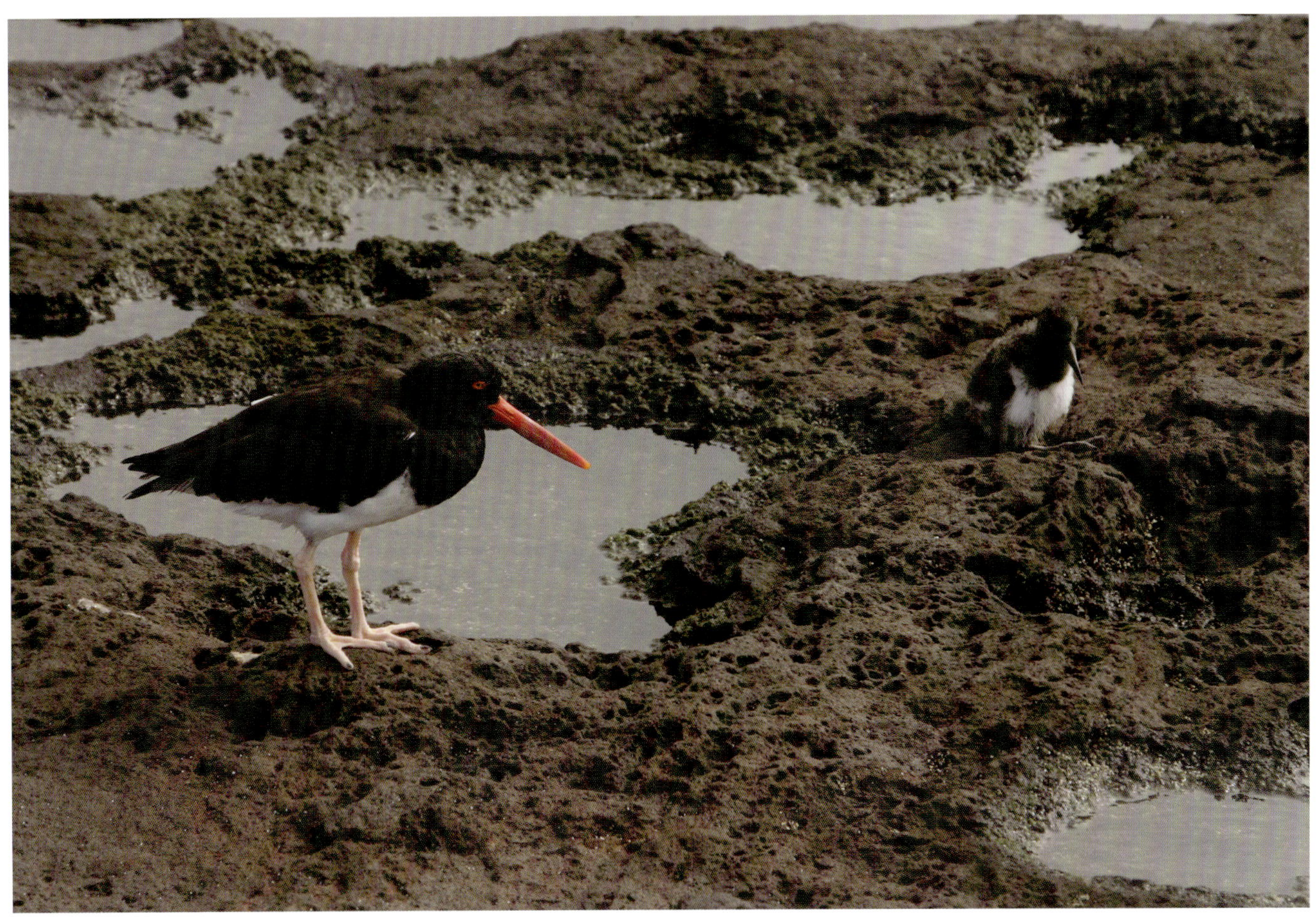

This juvenile Brown Pelican dives for fish.

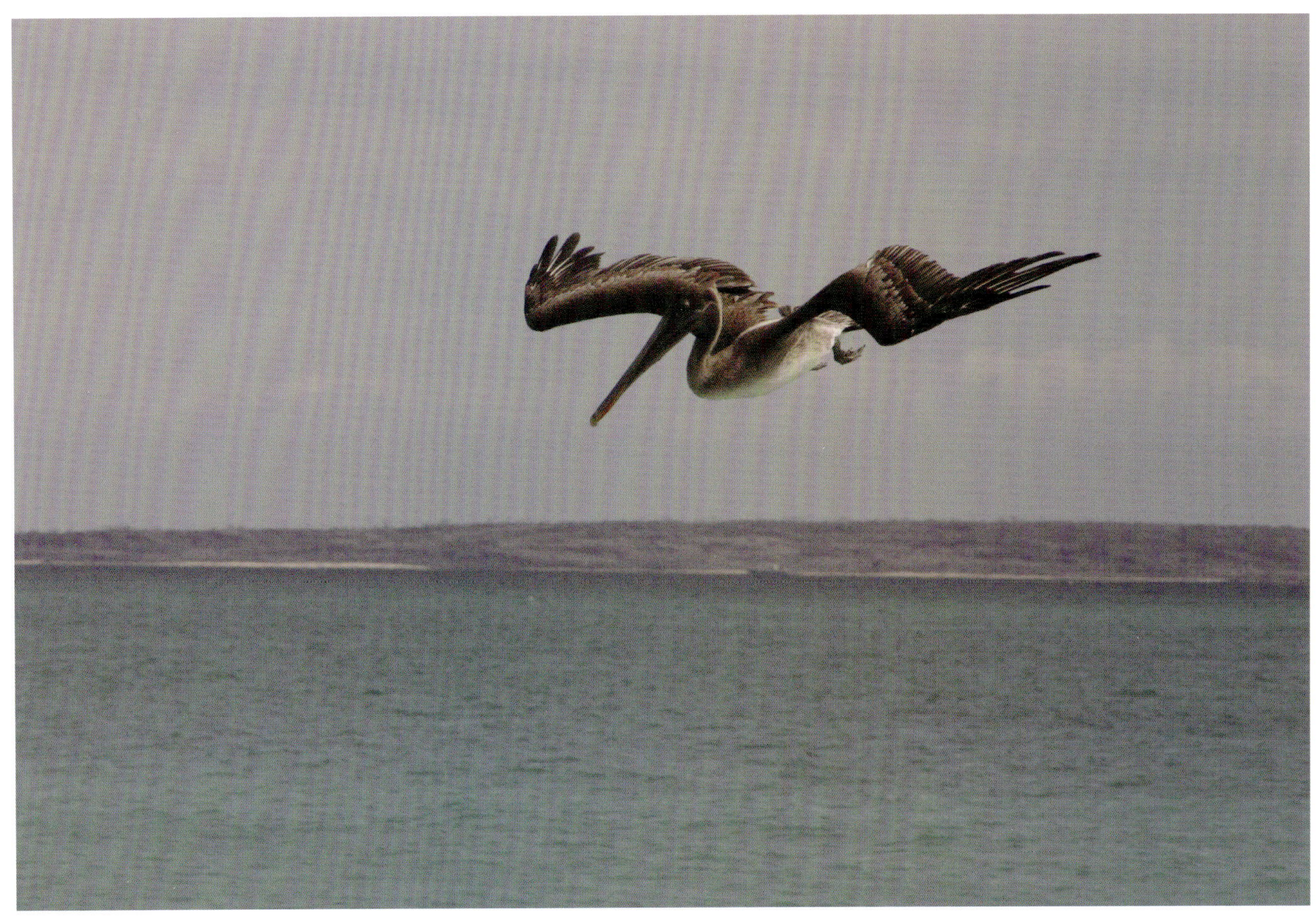

And this one takes a swim.

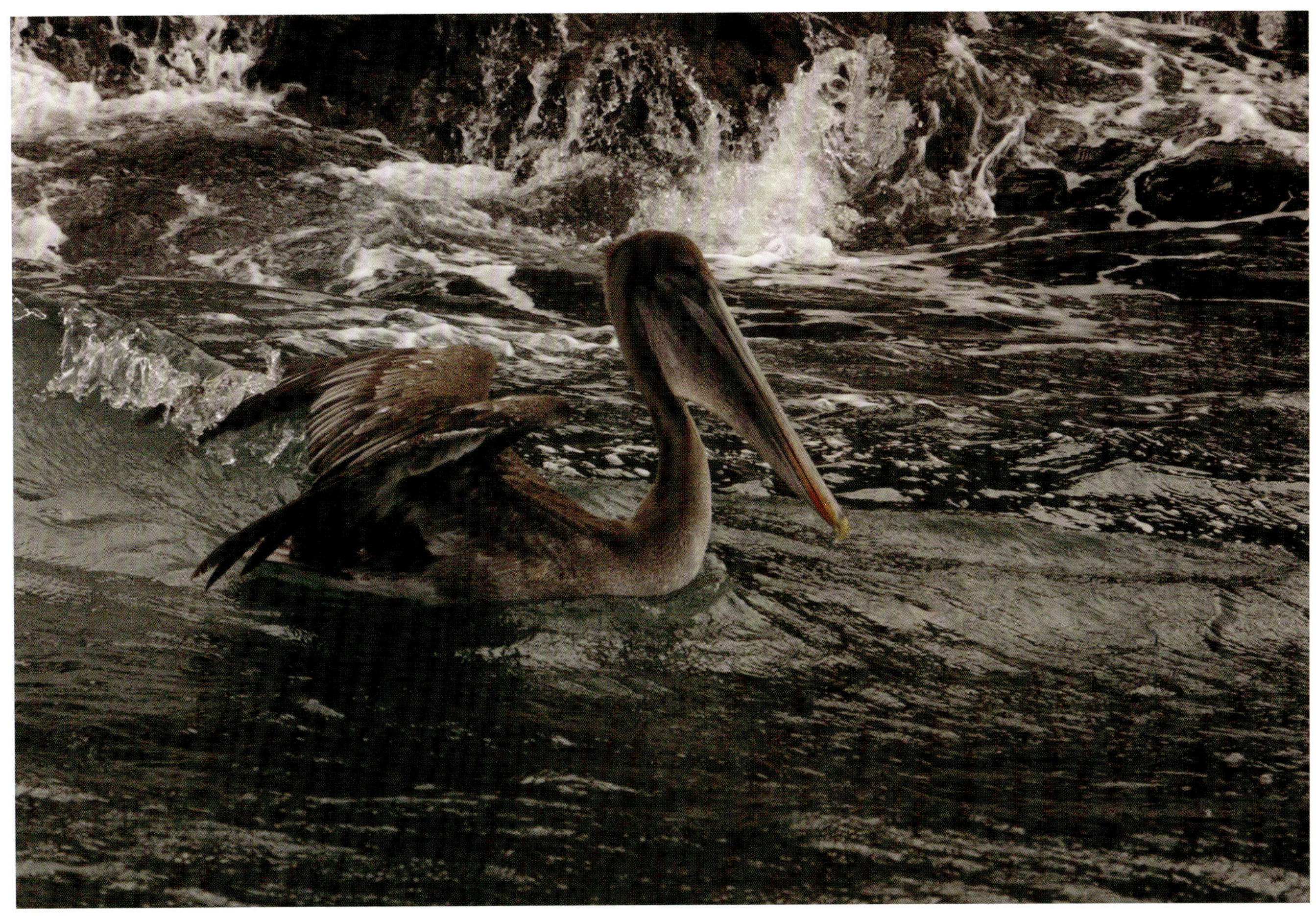

As do the White-cheeked Pintails.

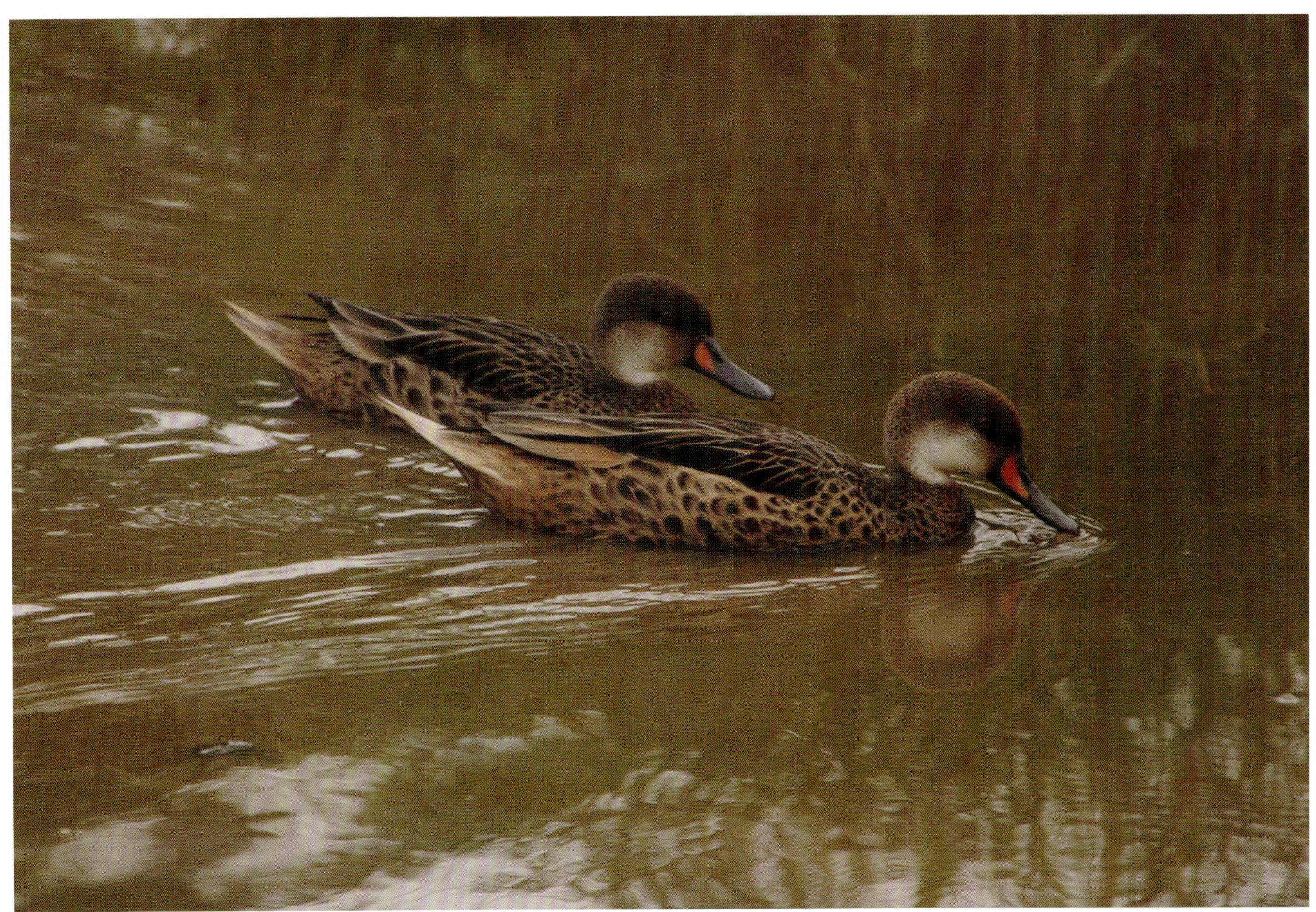

A Galapagos Penguin adult (left) and a juvenile perch on a cliff.

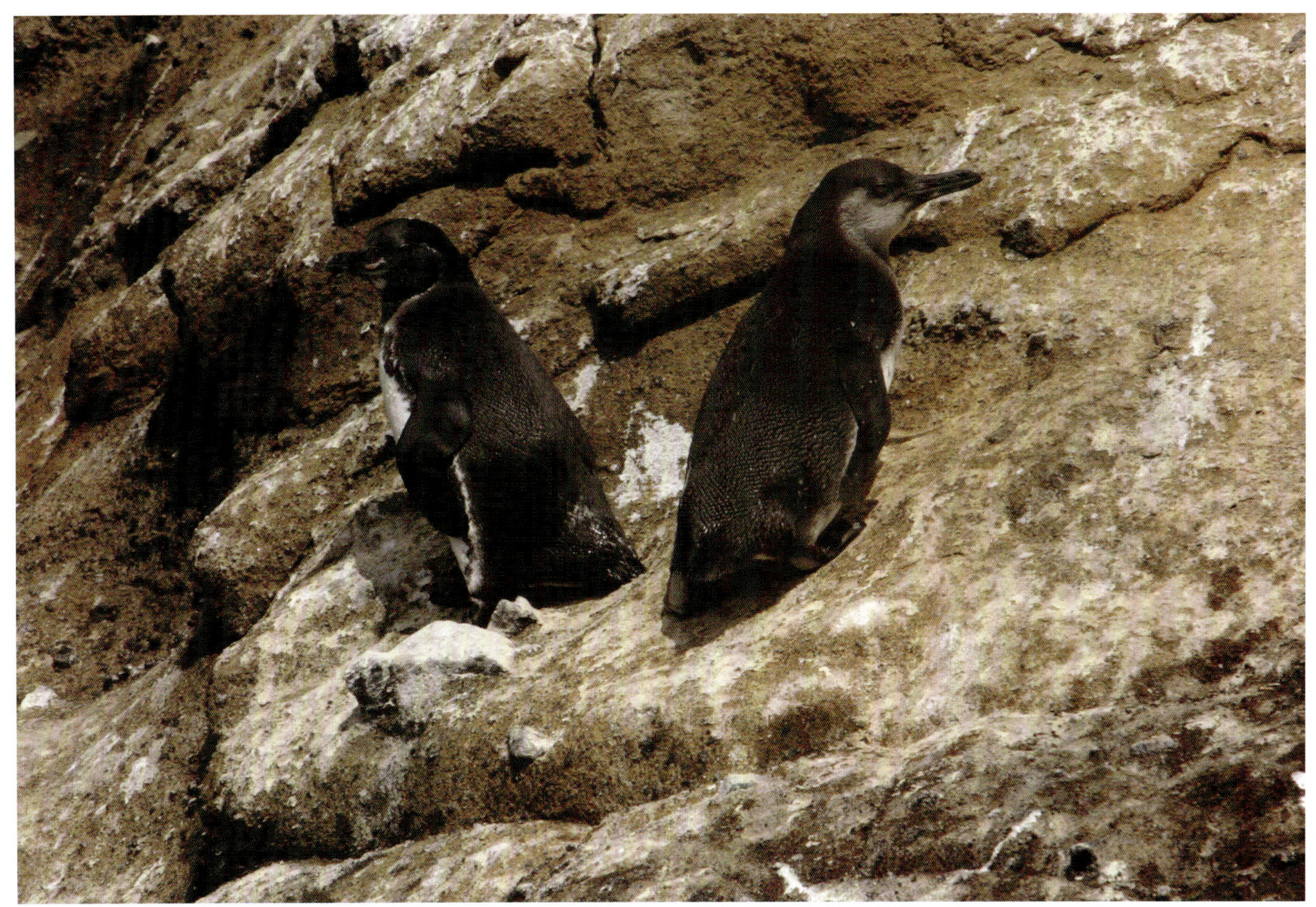

As do the Brown Noddies.

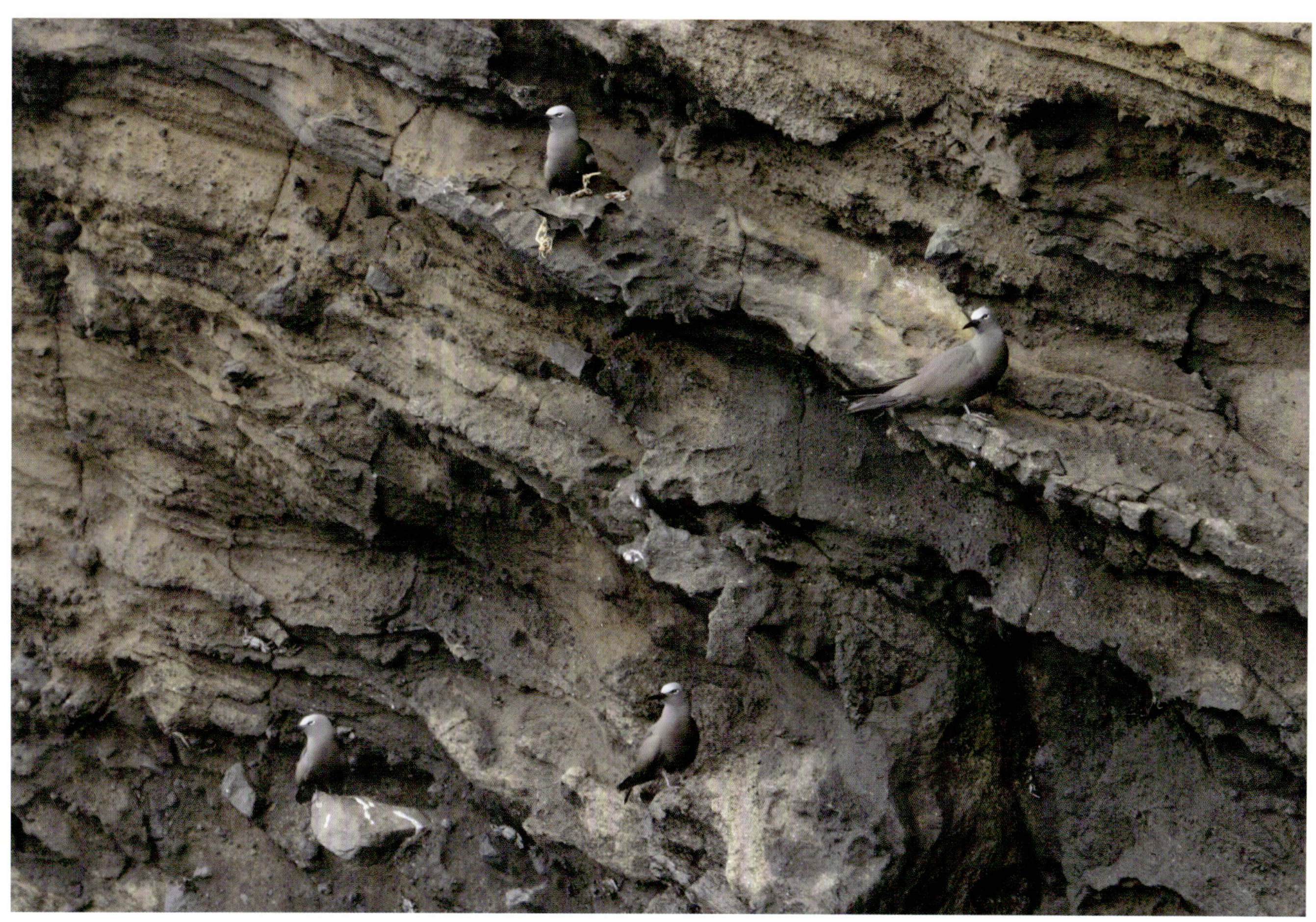

The Ruddy Turnstones poke around the shore.

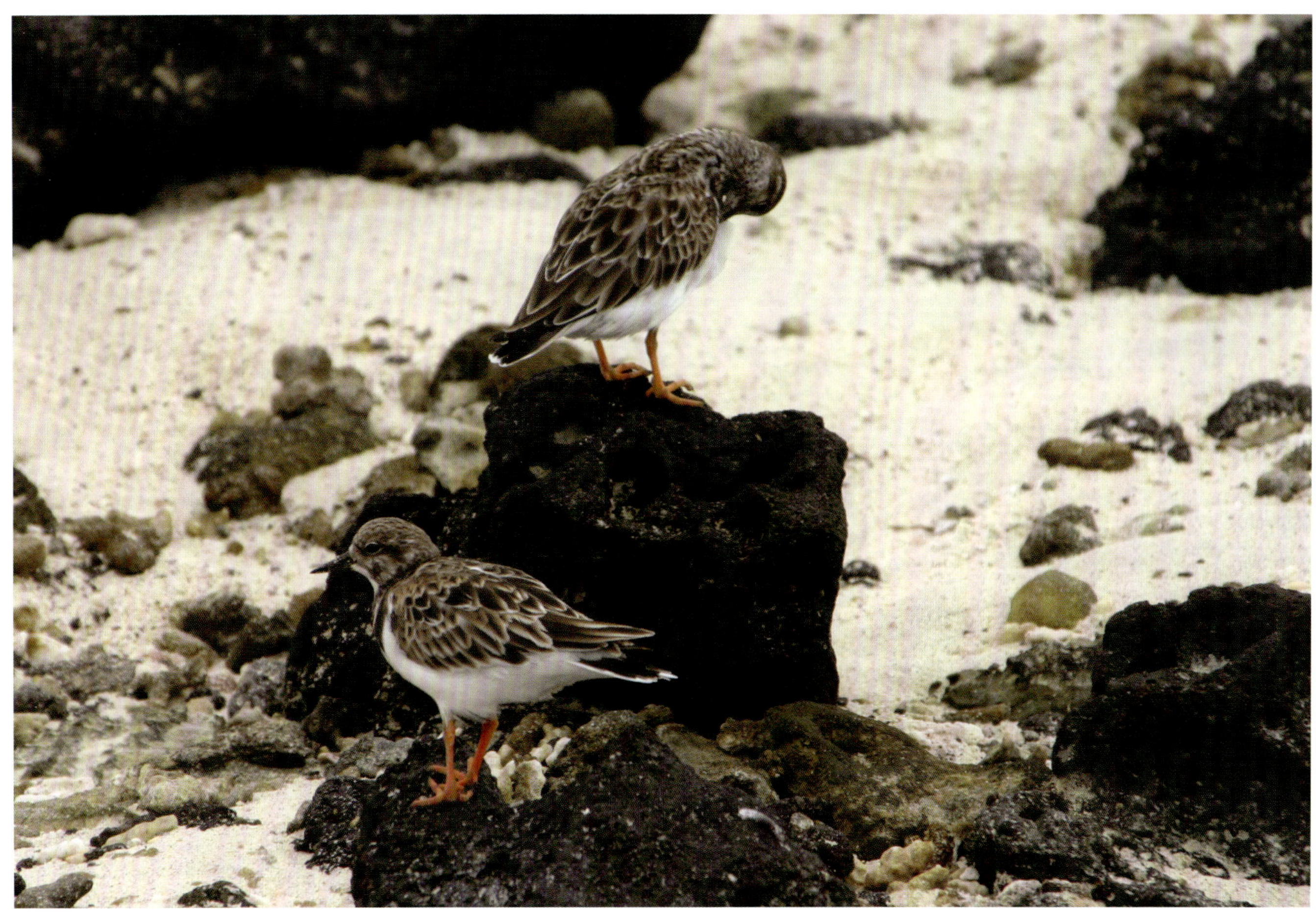

The Great Blue Heron looks out at the water.

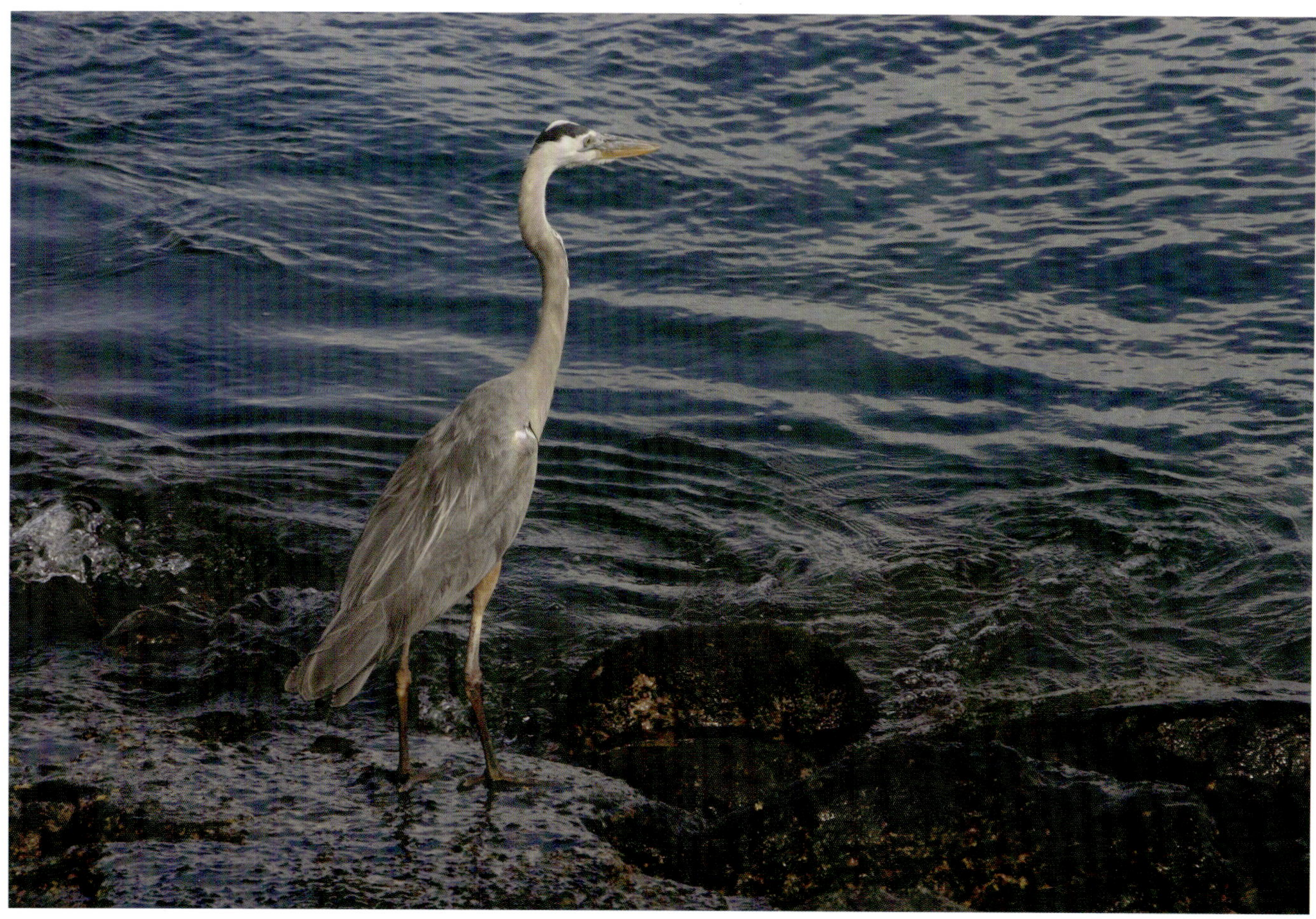

And the Vermillion Flycatcher takes flight in the highland forest.

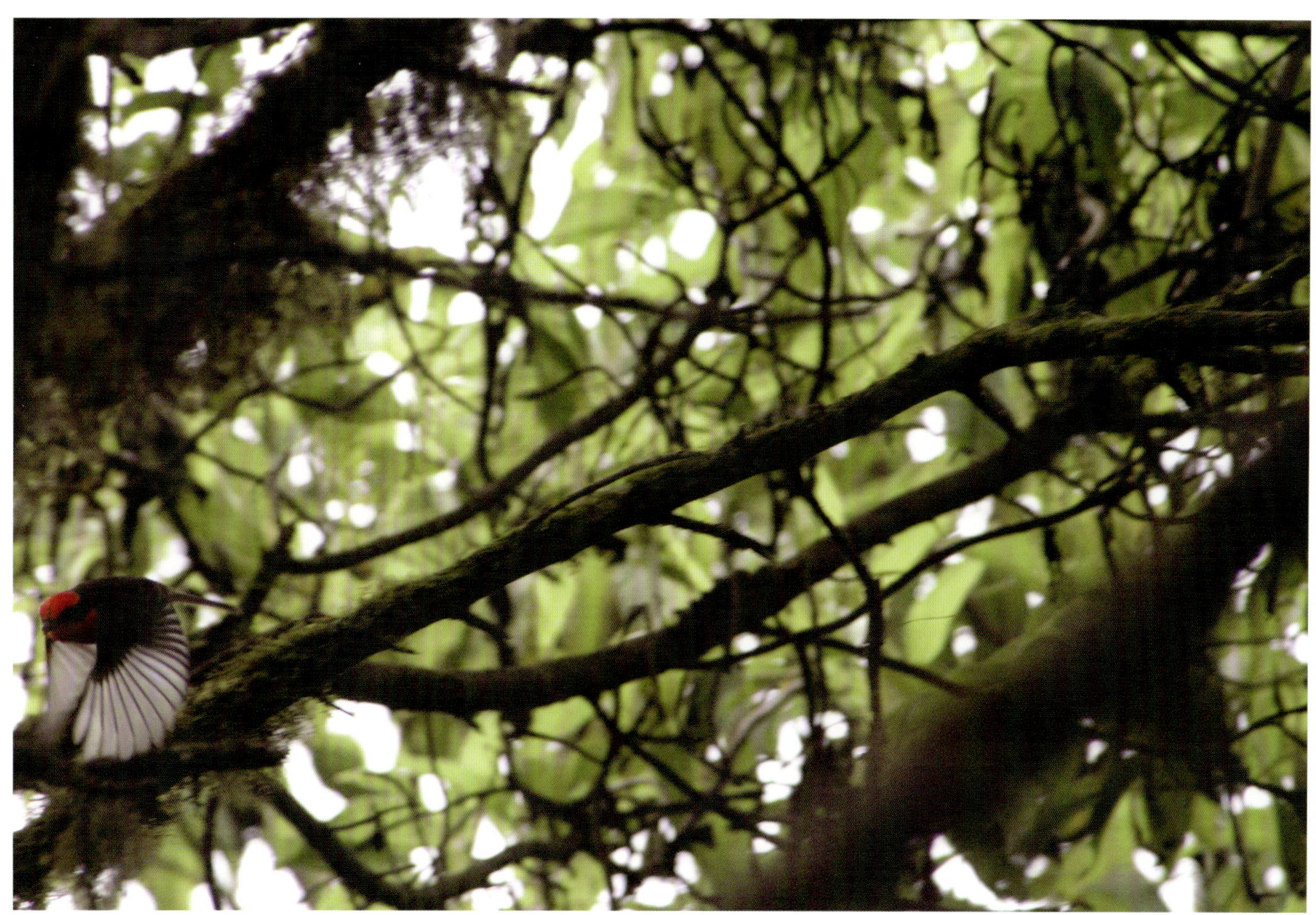

Just another day in the Galapagos.

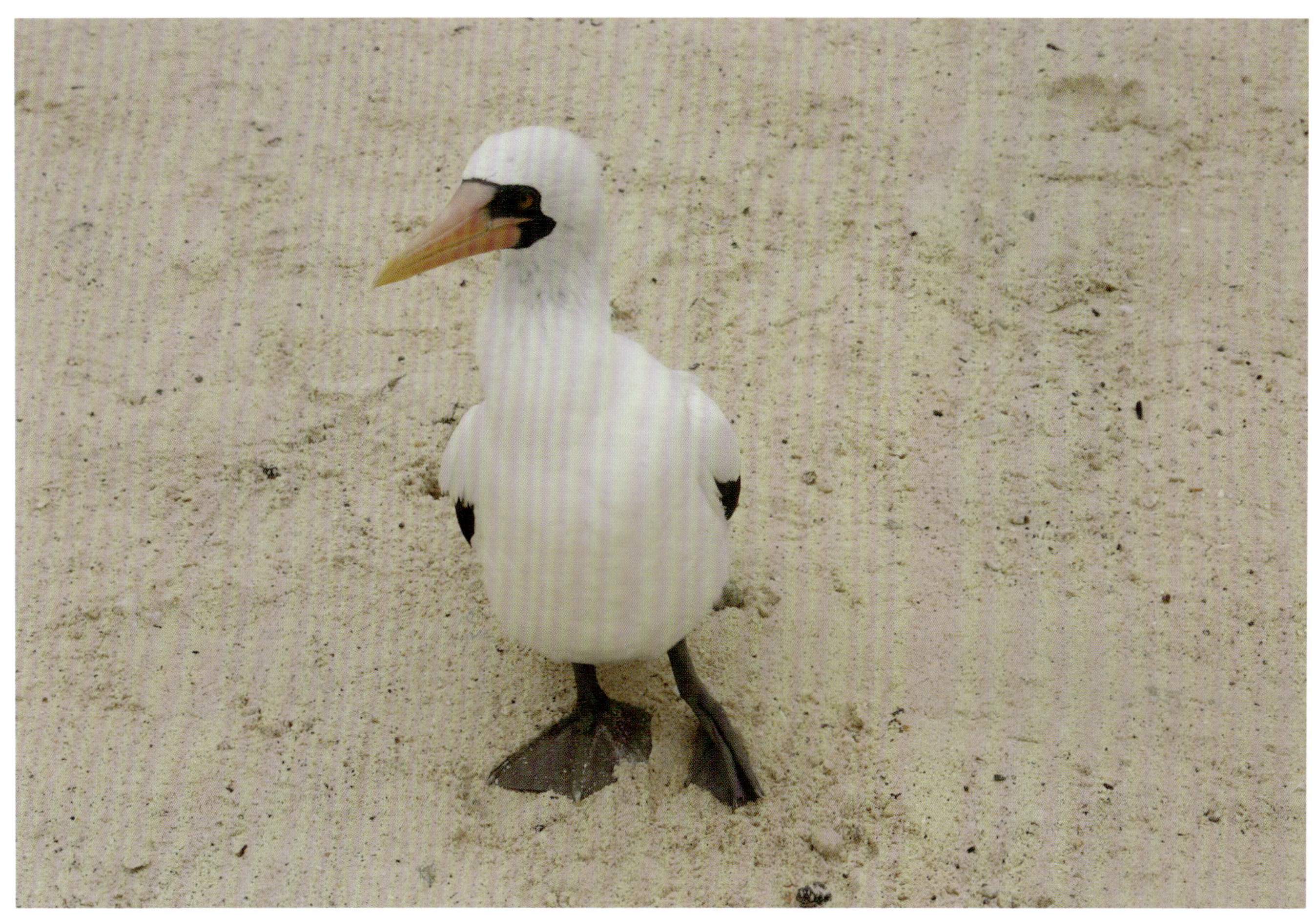

Nazca Booby

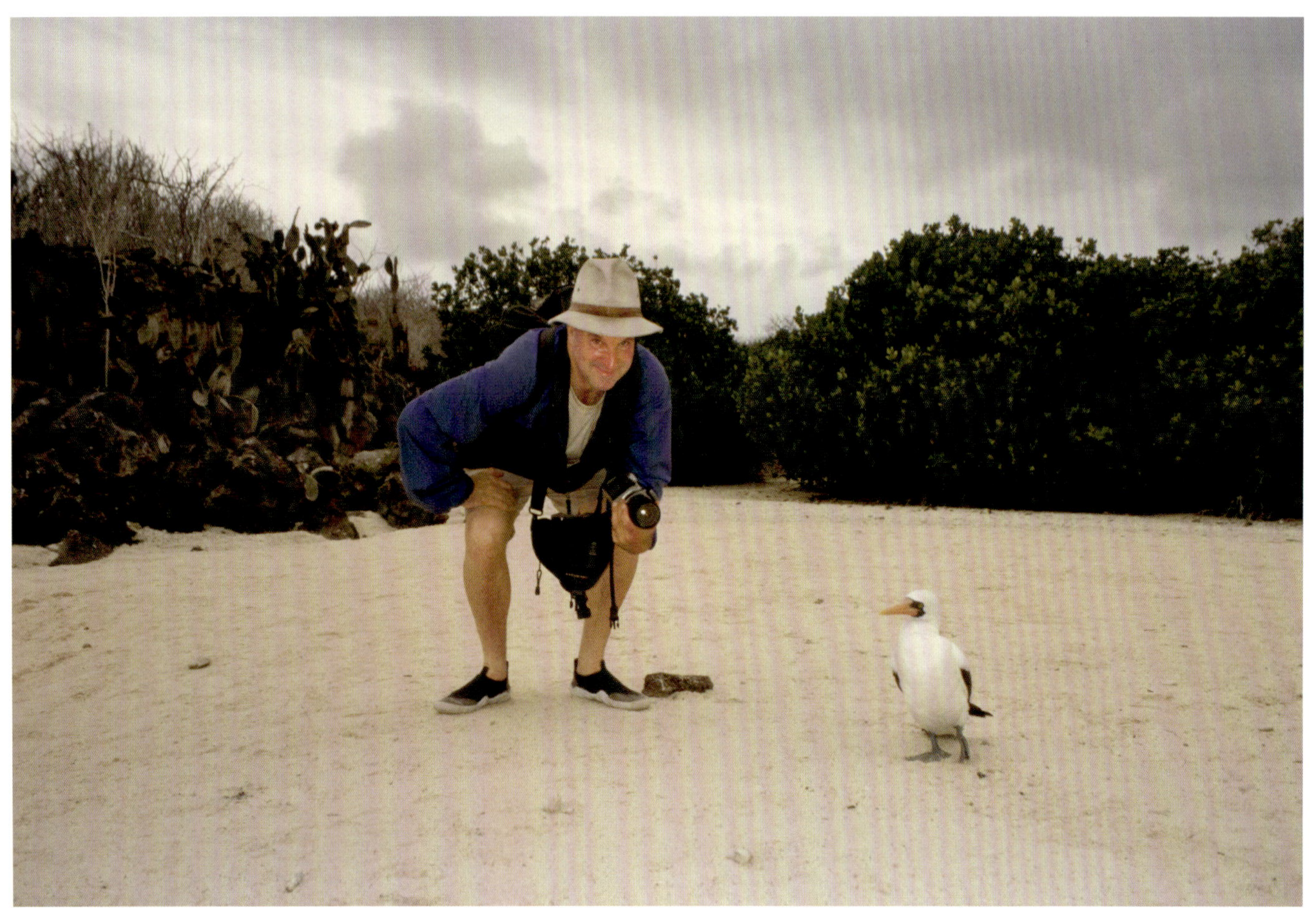

Afterword

The Galapagos Islands lie off the coast of Ecuador in South America. They were formed by erupted volcanoes millions of years ago. They are home to creatures such as the Land Iguana and Marine Iguana, the Galapagos Sea Lion, the Pacific Green Turtle, and the Galapagos Giant Tortoise. But the Galapagos also has birds—fabulous birds. It has boobies: Red-footed, Blue-footed, and Nazca. It has frigatebirds: Magnificent and Great. It has Waved Albatrosses, Lava Herons, Yellow-crowned Night-Herons, and the majestic Galapagos Hawk. The tiny Sanderling and Yellow Warbler flit about in the spiny shrubbery and trot over rocks that were left by the volcanoes. The Swallow-tailed Gull—with a red ring around his eye—and the American Oystercatcher—with his orange beak—also live on these islands. There are

Author photograph by Patience Fish Tekulsky: Mathew Tekulsky and Nazca Booby, Darwin Bay, Tower Island, 12/20/04

Afterword

four species of mockingbirds: Galapagos, Charles, Hood, and Chatham. And then there are the finches: Tree, Ground, Cactus, and Vegetarian Finches—which Charles Darwin observed in 1835 and used to develop his theory of evolution.

Many of the birds in the Galapagos live nowhere else on earth. They have adapted to life on these islands, and some of them only exist on one particular island. They have very few natural enemies and they have no fear of people, so you can walk right up and take their photograph or even talk to them. Some of the Galapagos birds are threatened with extinction, so it is very important that we protect these marvelous creatures. They are so beautiful, and they do so many interesting things—like eating yellow flowers, blowing up their red pouches, or clicking their beaks together, as you have seen.

I hope that you have enjoyed this photographic voyage to see the birds of the Galapagos Islands as much as I have enjoyed creating these images.

List of Plates

All of the bird photographs in this book were taken with a Canon EOS Digital Rebel camera and a Tamron AF 28-300mm Ultra Zoom F/3.5-6.3 LD Aspherical XR [IF] Macro (Model A06) lens.

55 Swallow-tailed Gulls, Darwin Bay, Tower Island, 12/20/04
130mm, ISO 1600, 1/250 second at f/7.1

57 Swallow-tailed Gulls, North Seymour Island, 12/21/04
300mm, ISO 800, 1/640 second at f/10

59 Juvenile Swallow-tailed Gull, Prince Philip's Steps, Tower Island, 12/20/04
300mm, ISO 1600, 1/500 second at f/9

61 Swallow-tailed Gulls, Darwin Bay, Tower Island, 12/20/04
42mm, ISO 400, 1/200 second at f/9

63 American Flamingos, Bachas Beach, Santa Cruz Island, 12/21/04
77mm, ISO 400, 1/640 second at f/13

65 American Flamingo, Bachas Beach, Santa Cruz Island, 12/21/04
300mm, ISO 100, 1/400 second at f/8

67 Vegetarian Finch and Yellow Cordia flower, Charles Darwin Research Station, Puerto Ayora, Santa Cruz Island, 12/24/04
300mm, ISO 800, 1/640 second at f/10

69 Vegetarian Finch and Yellow Cordia flower, Charles Darwin Research Station, Puerto Ayora, Santa Cruz Island, 12/24/04
300mm, ISO 800, 1/640 second at f/10

71 Galapagos Mockingbird, Darwin Bay, Tower Island, 12/20/04
300mm, ISO 800, 1/640 second at f/9

73 Galapagos Mockingbird and Galapagos Giant Tortoise, Charles Darwin Research Station, Puerto Ayora, Santa Cruz Island, 12/24/04
55mm, ISO 800, 1/200 second at f/8

75 Yellow Warbler and Galapagos Giant Tortoise, Rancho Primicias, Santa Cruz Island, 12/24/04
300mm, ISO 1600, 1/640 second at f/9

77 Lava Heron, Puerto Egas, Santiago Island, 12/23/04
300mm, ISO 800, 1/500 second at f/8

79 Lava Heron, Puerto Egas, Santiago Island, 12/23/04
300mm, ISO 1600, 1/800 second at f/10

81 Juvenile Lava Heron, Puerto Egas, Santiago Island, 12/23/04
300mm, ISO 1600, 1/640 second at f/10

83 Yellow-crowned Night-Heron, Punta Suarez, Hood Island, 12/25/04
168mm, ISO 1600, 1/500 second at f/10

85 Waved Albatrosses, Punta Suarez, Hood Island, 12/25/04
200mm, ISO 800, 1/800 second at f/11

87 Waved Albatrosses, Punta Suarez, Hood Island, 12/25/04
168mm, ISO 800, 1/800 second at f/11

89 Waved Albatrosses, Punta Suarez, Hood Island, 12/25/04
168mm, ISO 800, 1/800 second at f/11

91 Juvenile Galapagos Hawk, Punta Suarez, Hood Island, 12/25/04
28mm, ISO 200, 1/500 second at f/11

93 Juvenile Galapagos Hawk, Punta Suarez, Hood Island, 12/25/04
119mm, ISO 800, 1/500 second at f/18

95 Sanderling, North Seymour Island, 12/21/04
300mm, ISO 400, 1/500 second at f/9

97 Hood Mockingbird, Punta Suarez, Hood Island, 12/25/04
130mm, ISO 400, 1/500 second at f/16

99 American Oystercatcher, Puerto Egas, Santiago Island, 12/23/04
300mm, ISO 1600, 1/640 second at f/10

101 American Oystercatcher chick, Puerto Egas, Santiago Island, 12/23/04
238mm, ISO 800, 1/500 second at f/9

103 American Oystercatcher and chick, Puerto Egas, Santiago Island, 12/23/04
109mm, ISO 400, 1/400 second at f/10

105 Juvenile Brown Pelican, Bachas Beach, Santa Cruz Island, 12/21/04
300mm, ISO 1600, 1/2000 second at f/16

107 Juvenile Brown Pelican, Tagus Cove, Isabela Island, 12/22/04
109mm, ISO 1600, 1/1000 second at f/16

109 White-cheeked Pintails, Rancho Primicias, Santa Cruz Island, 12/24/04
300mm, ISO 800, 1/640 second at f/10

111 Galapagos Penguin adult and juvenile, Tagus Cove, Isabela Island, 12/22/04
168mm, ISO 1600, 1/1600 second at f/18

113 Brown Noddies, Tagus Cove, Isabela Island, 12/22/04
84mm, ISO 1600, 1/250 second at f/8

115 Ruddy Turnstones, Darwin Bay, Tower Island, 12/20/04
209mm, ISO 800, 1/500 second at f/9

117 Great Blue Heron, Puerto Baquerizo Moreno, San Cristobal Island, 12/26/04
119mm, ISO 800, 1/640 second at f/13

119 Vermillion Flycatcher, Santa Cruz Island, 12/24/04
300mm, ISO 800, 1/500 second at f/8

121 Nazca Booby, Darwin Bay, Tower Island, 12/20/04
59mm, ISO 400, 1/500 second at f/13

About the Author

Mathew Tekulsky is the author of *Backyard Bird Photography* and *The Art of Hummingbird Gardening*, among other books. He is also the author of "The Birdman of Bel Air," a column on NationalGeographic.com that featured essays and photographs about his birding experiences. His bird photographs have been published in field guides such as the *National Geographic Field Guide to Birds: California* and the *Smithsonian Field Guide to the Birds of North America*. His bird photographs have also been exhibited in galleries and museums, including the Roger Tory Peterson Institute of Natural History.

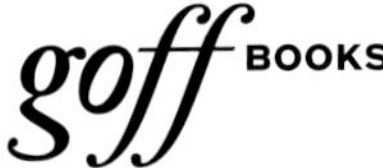

Published by Goff Books, an Imprint of ORO Editions.
Executive publisher: Gordon Goff.

www.goffbooks.com
info@goffbooks.com

Graphic Design: Rita Sowins / Sowins Design
Goff Books Project Coordinator: Kirby Anderson

10 9 8 7 6 5 4 3 2 1 First Edition

Library of Congress data available upon request. World Rights: available.

ISBN: 978-1-951541-12-5

Color separations and printing: ORO Group Ltd.
Printed in China.

International distribution: www.goffbooks.com/distribution

FRONT COVER: Blue-footed Booby, North Seymour Island, 12/21/04

FRONTISPIECE: Red-footed Booby, Darwin Bay, Tower Island, 12/20/04

BACK COVER PHOTO: Author photograph by Patience Fish Tekulsky: Mathew Tekulsky and juvenile Blue-footed Booby, Playa Ochoa, San Cristobal Island, 12/19/04